They worked all their lives

To Mom and Granny Wood

Carl Chinn

They worked all their lives

Women of the urban poor in England, 1880–1939

Manchester University Press

Manchester and New York

Distributed exclusively in North America by St. Martin's Press Inc.

Copyright © Carl Chinn 1988

Published by Manchester University Press
Oxford Road, Manchester M13 9PL, UK

*Distributed exclusively in the USA and Canada
by* St. Martin's Press, Inc.,
175 Fifth Avenue, New York, NY 10010, USA

British Library cataloguing in publication data
Chinn, Carl
    They worked all their lives : women of
    the urban poor in England, 1880–1939.
    1. Working-class women—England—Social
    life and customs 2. City and town life—
    England—History
    I. Title
    942.082′0880′623   HQ1593

Library of Congress cataloging in publication data
Chinn, Carl
    They worked all their lives : women of the urban poor in England,
    1880–1939 / by Carl Chinn.
      p.   cm.
    Bibliography : p. 169.
    Includes index.
    ISBN 0–7190–2436–6 : $35.00 (est.)
    1. Women, Poor—England—History. 2. Urban women—England—
    History. 3. Urban poor—England—History. I. Title.
    HQ 1599.E5C47   1988
    305.4′2′0942—dc 19   87–36701

ISBN 0–7190–2436–6 hardback

Typeset in Great Britain
by Megaron, Cardiff, Wales

Printed in Great Britain by
Billing & Sons Ltd, Worcester

Contents

Acknowledgements

Preface   xi

Introduction   1

Chapter one: A hidden matriarchy   12

Chapter two: The power of mothers   45

Chapter three: Independent women   84

Chapter four: Survival   133

Chapter five: Fighting back   155

Notes   167

Sources   169

Index   181

. . . the wise man recognises that the real acting authority in daily life is that of the woman.

Helen Bosanquet, *The Family*, p.273

Acknowledgements

Any book is not solely the product of the writer; it is also the result of the help, inspiration and advice of others. In this connection, I should like first to thank Dorothy Thompson who read various drafts of this book and offered criticism and assistance throughout its writing. Without her support in the past this book would not have been written. Secondly, I should like to thank my family and friends for their constant encouragement, particularly my wife Kay; my mother and father, Sylvia and Buck; my brother Darryl, and Mrs Anne Masefield who was ever ready to act as my typist. Specific thanks are also due to those people who have provided oral evidence for this book and a list of their names appears under the sources; to Dr Hugh McLeod of Birmingham University for his help with my research; to the staff in the Local Studies and Archives Departments of the City of Birmingham Central Reference Library for their assistance, and to Roy Palmer for the date of 'Pal of My Cradle Days'. To all those who have helped in one way or another, my deepest thanks.

Preface

In the Preface to *The Making of the English Working Class*, Edward Thompson sounded out a clarion call for social history when he declared that it was his intention to rescue the poor stockinger, the Luddite cropper, the obsolete handloom weaver, the utopian artisan, and even the deluded follower of Joanna Southcote, from the enormous condescension of posterity. In his wake, the battle-cry of the social historian surely has become 'Enter the blind alleys! Remember the lost causes! Do not forget the losers!' Over the last twenty years, inspired by this call-to-arms, social historians have sought to expand our knowledge of the past and our understanding of the forces which affect societies, communities and individuals. Numerous studies have been written looking at history, in the words of Harvey Kaye, from 'the bottom up'. No longer is our view of the past 'top-heavy', restricted to analysing the actions and the lives of the rulers and the decision-makers of a society or era. Instead, the balance has begun to be redressed by social historians who believe that the study of the weakest, the poorest, and the most oppressed in any society is at least as significant as the study of the powerful.

This book belongs firmly in that category which wishes to shed light on those who have been forgotten or neglected in historical research, but it is also influenced by a more recent phenomenon, the rapid growth in women's history. As with social history, the result of new and innovative research has been a broadening of the horizons of historical inquiry, this time in a way which leads to a realisation of, and an emphasis on, the importance and significance of women in the past. Admirable and much-needed work, by writers such as Jill Liddington, Jill Norris, Angela V. John, Martha Vicinus, Andro Linklater, Leonore Davidoff and others, has been important in this respect. Yet it remains true – for reasons relating to both the quantity and the quality of the evidence available – that much research concerned with women's history, in common with social history, has concentrated on the more articulate and better organised of 'the forgotten': the skilled of the working class and the women of the middle class; trade-unionists and female suffragists.

In 1973, Peter N. Stearns wrote an article entitled 'Working-class women in Britain', which appeared in *Suffer and Be Still: Women in the Victorian Age*, edited by Martha Vicinus. He noted that women's history had a tendency to concentrate on women of public achievement, especially feminists, whilst studies on working-class women referred mainly to their position in industry. More recently, there have been attempts to rectify this imbalance, notably by Standish Meacham in his valuable study, *A Life Apart: The English Working Class 1890–1914*. His examination of the lives led by working-class women, and his attention to their relevance to their communities, has been expanded and enhanced by the researchers of Elizabeth Roberts. Through a skilful use of oral history, she has pioneered work relating to their day-to-day lives. In the process she has indicated the crucial position women held within the English working class. Still, little has been written specifically concerning the poor of English society and, with the exception of three excellent articles by Ellen Ross relating to London, even less has been written about the women of the urban poor. It is the aim of this book to provide, for the first time, a comprehensive and detailed study of the way of life and importance of these women, and by so doing to fill a gap in our knowledge of the recent past.

Introduction

There exist two main difficulties in writing a book which concentrates on the urban poor. The first is the fact that, to many historians, they appear as an almost amorphous group, difficult to quantify and to distinguish statistically from the rest of the working class. Despite the fact that it is almost impossible to given an absolute and all-embracing definition of who were the urban poor, it is true that this section existed and was identified and written about by astute social observers in the period 1880–1939. C. F. G. Masterman – a Liberal advocate of social reform – stated in 1901 in *The Heart Of The Empire. Discussions of Problems of Modern City Life in England* that fundamental divisions were apparent amongst the working class, and that the 'artisan', or skilled man, could not be confounded with the labourer or the casual worker as one of the poor. As a commentator on the Birmingham working class put it:

We have spoken of the labour *middle* class. There is an upper and a lower stratum, too; for not only does society at large resolve into the three great divisions we know as upper, middle, and lower classes, but each of these again separates itself into minor subdivisions ...
Between the aristocracy of industry and the unfortunate herd who crowd the lowest rungs of the ladder there is a very wide gulf.[1]

This kind of social observer discerned that an insufficient and often irregular income differentiated the unskilled and their families from the more prosperous of the working class. They also recognised that, whilst economic circumstances were crucial in creating that division, it was made more potent by environmental and cultural factors.

Who, then, were the urban poor? Charles Booth in *Life and Labour of the People in London* – the initial volume of which was published in 1889 – was the first investigator to try and answer this question in a detailed and statistical fashion. At the beginning of his seventeen-volume survey he had expected that his research would disprove the claim made by H. M. Hyndman – a Socialist and leader of the Social Democratic Federation – that twenty-five per cent of the people of London were living in extreme poverty. In fact, Booth found that thirty per cent of the capital's population was living below a poverty line which he set at an income of between eighteen and twenty shillings a week for a 'moderate' family. He divided the capital's inhabitants into eight groups which were based on family earnings. The poor encompassed Classes A to D and, apart from those who were better-paid and whose unwise deployment of their wages reduced them to poverty, they were characterised by the fact that their heads of household did not possess the skills which were necessary to secure regular employment. Women were more severely affected by this problem than were men, with the result that widows or deserted women made up a significantly large contingent of the 100,000 people (eleven per cent of the total) who were included in Class B, the very poor. At the turn of the century, Booth's findings received statistical validation and were given a national relevance by a study made by Seebohm Rowntree in York. His research, carried out at a time of reasonable prosperity, was published under the title *Poverty. A Study of Town Life*. It showed that the capital was not unusual in its number of poor people, for Rowntree indicated that nearly twenty-eight per cent of the population of York was living below the poverty line. This he set at an income of 21s 8d a week for a labourer, his wife and three children. Such a figure, Rowntree believed, was capable of maintaining that family only in a state of mere 'physical efficiency'; that is, it precluded all expenditure on what might be termed 'the quality of life'.

When examining the statistical evidence provided by Booth, it is necessary to be aware, as Ellen Ross points out, that many families in his largest group – the 377,000 people (forty per cent of the total) who made up Class E – could readily descend from their situation of regular standard earnings into one of irregular earnings and poverty. Singly or in combination, the death, illness, injury or unemployment of the chief wage-earner, as well as the onset of old age, were all factors which could drastically and adversely affect a family's economic position and social standing. The recognition of the presence and influence of this 'poverty cycle', whereby circumstance could lead to a family moving in and out of a state of privation during the course of the years, was one of the most important of Rowntree's conclusions. In particular, he showed how the life of a labourer was marked by five alternating periods of want and plenty. During early childhood he lived in poverty, from which he would rise as he and his siblings began work. After marriage, the birth of children would once again thrust him back into distress, which would then be alleviated as his children in turn became wage-earners. Finally, as his children married and left home, he would, for the last time, become impoverished. Rowntree also noted the disturbing fact that women were in poverty during the greater part of the time in which they bore children.

The urban poor, then, did not belong to a closed caste. In an age when the state made little provision for those who suffered misfortune, the family of the skilled man could easily be reduced to an existence of acute need. This fact was particularly obvious in the North of England during the depression of the inter-war years. Before 1914, unemployment had been largely discriminatory in its effects; during the 1920s and 1930s, like illness and injury, it became a hazard which could as easily afflict the skilled as the unskilled. At the same time, it is important to be aware of an issue not fully addressed by Rowntree; that of the inability of many of the urban poor to escape, even temporarily, from their situation. The cycle which he identified was a concept which was not applicable to all. Poverty was the birthright of the many, and escape from its shackles was precluded by disability, ill-health, lack of education, intermittent employment, and above all the inequalities inherent in an often unfair and uncaring society. Moreover, both Booth and Rowntree made allowance in their figures only for moderate-sized families. As shall be examined in a later chapter, many families of the urban poor were not moderate in their size; they were large and, consequently, would always remain in poverty. Although there was certainly movement in and out of the ranks

of the urban poor, without doubt there existed this hereditary
aspect to their position of deprivation, an aspect that was made
particularly potent by the manner in which their way of life
differed in significant respects from that of the rest of the
working class. Consequently, I would argue that, in the period
covered by this study and during which various economic
determinants of poverty were relevant, some individuals and
families who were monetarily poor might culturally appertain
to the upper working class, and, of course, the reverse can also
be true. I would affirm, then, that the urban poor as discussed in
this book were distinguished as a separate section of the
working class as much by their cultural distinctiveness as they
were by their impoverishment.

This argument is one which I propounded in detail in my
doctoral thesis, 'The anatomy of a working-class neighbourhood: West Sparkbrook 1871–1914'. Whilst the urban working
class of England was not an amalgam of working classes,
neither was it a monolithic whole, and this district of
Birmingham provided evidence from a variety of sources of the
pervasive manner in which variations in life-styles ensured and
strengthened its economic stratification. The emphatic social
separation of the 'cultural' urban poor from mainstream
working-class life was exhibited in numerous ways. From their
shopping habits to their politics; from their definition of what
was 'rough' and what was respectable to their attitudes towards
drinking, gambling and fighting, and even from their schooling
to the responsibilities of their children, the differentiation
between the 'cultural' urban poor and the more affluent of the
working class was obvious. More decisive and important than
all these, the distinctiveness of the urban poor was at its most
apparent in respect of the position and role of women. It is for
this reason that they provide the subject of this study.

A second difficulty encountered with regard to this study is that
connected with the various types of evidence available.
Descriptions of the way of life and living standards of the urban
poor by contemporary upper- and middle-class social observers
and novelists are plentiful, although they are often scattered
amongst studies or novels about the working class in general. It
has been necessary to bring this evidence together and, at the

same time, to bear in mind an important proviso as to its use, made by John Burnett in his introduction to *Useful Toil: Autobiographies of Working People from the 1820s to the 1920s.* That is, that whilst the surveys of these private investigators supply the researcher with a mass of detailed evidence, the writers themselves were a stage removed from the individuals with whom they dealt. This fact was readily accepted by Gwendolen Freeman, the author of *The Houses Behind. Sketches of a Birmingham Back Street.* In her book she described her experiences, during the 1930s, as an insurance collector in the notorious and very poor Summer Lane neighbourhood of Birmingham. She admitted that she could lay no claim to knowing intimately the people she described, and she acknow-ledged that, because she spoke 'lawn-tennis', she would never be treated by them as a crony; she would always be divided from them by language, background and experience of life.

The studies of the social explorers, then, were not written by members of the working class, nor were they written for a working-class readership. They were undertaken by and for those who belonged to another class. No matter how well-meaning and concerned these writers were, they were inevit-ably influenced in their comments by their birth, social standing and cultural affinities. This does not invalidate either their findings or their observations, both of which constitute precious material for the social historian. Indeed, as Gwendolen Freeman understood, advantages accrued from the detachment of the investigators from the subjects of their inquiries. In her opinion, precisely because she was not one of them, she could hear many confidences. The outsider could benefit in other ways, and this is reflected particularly in the invaluable statistical and factual evidence which the social explorers so painstakingly provided. It is also apparent in the awareness they arouse in their readers of the dismal and life-destroying environment in which the urban poor lived. Still, caution must be exercised when using these investigations as a source, and this is particularly necessary in respect of the 'impressionistic' evidence. When an investigator or novelist concentrates on the 'feel' of the slums and their dwellers, then the social separation induced by their belonging to another class can become a chasm.

Some of the most interesting and important examples of this genre appear in a book of extracts edited by Peter Keating entitled *Into Unknown England 1866–1913. Selections From The Social Explorers*. This title aptly sums up the attitude and aims of those impressionistic writers included in the book who regarded themselves as intrepid explorers entering an unknown continent which was made up of the slums of urban England. Earlier in the century, writers such as Henry Mayhew (in *London Labour and the London Poor*) had also made use of the image that the slums were 'unknown territory' which needed to be 'opened up', so that those who dwelt in them could be made accessible to the uplifting effects of civilised society. However, it was the 1880s which were to witness the full flowering of this descriptive form. George Sims set the tone in 1883 when he explained that his study, *How the Poor Live*, was a 'book of travel'. In it he described the urban poor as 'wild races'; not only did they live in a 'dark continent' but they required the attention of missionaries as much as did foreign tribes who inhabited more distant lands. Seven years later William Booth, the founder of the Salvation Army, exaggerated this imagery by explicitly comparing the perils of 'Darkest England' and its inhabitants to those of 'Darkest Africa'. His book, appropriately entitled *In Darkest England and the Way Out*, introduced terminologies and comparisons which were to become the vogue for a kind of social explorer. This type regarded the slums as an 'inferno', a hell peopled by a physically and morally degenerate race. Jack London, in *The People of The Abyss* (published in 1903), regarded the urban poor as the 'inefficients' of society, an opinon shared by George Gissing. In his novel, *The Nether World*, published in 1889, the children of the urban poor were described as 'bald, red-eyed, doughy-limbed abortions . . . hapless spawn of diseased humanity, born to embitter and brutalise yet further the lot of those who unwillingly gave them life'.[2] This 'new race' of short-statured, excitable and voluble English persons was lacking in stamina and was regarded as 'deteriorated stock'. The widespread acceptance of this view amongst the upper and middle classes, and the belief that the future of the nation and its position as a world-leader was jeopardised because of the 'inferior' character of the urban poor, so affected the govern-

ment that in 1904 it felt it necessary to set up an Inter-
Departmental Committee on Physical Deterioration.

It must always be remembered, then, that most social investigators were viewing the slums – quite naturally – in a very
different light from that of their inhabitants. They were
righteously shocked and disturbed by what they saw in the
'ghetto', 'the abyss', 'the jungle' or whatever other term or
phrase they used to evoke the image of an infernal region, a
place of the damned. Consequently, in the case of some, their
justifiable horror at the living conditions of the poor extended
to a horror of the poor themselves. As Walter Allen remarked in
his introduction to the Everyman edition of *The Nether World*,
Gissing did not really like the working class, and this is a theme
amplified by Benny Green. Writing in the introduction to the
Oxford University Press edition of Clarence Rook's *The
Hooligan Nights*, he bemoaned the fact that, with the exception
of the novelist Arthur Morrison, social observers had failed to
grasp the simple proposition that the working class was neither
more nor less virtuous than any other class, it was simply
poorer. In his opinion, the working class was either
'sentimentalised by the guiltwracked or stigmatised by the
pietistic'.[3]

It would be easy on the impressionistic evidence alone to
condemn the urban poor as insensitive, immoral, joyless and
unhappy, destined to lead lives doomed to despair and
despondency. Those of the middle class who worked regularly
amongst them knew this was not necessarily so. In *The Married
Working Woman. A Study*, published in 1911 by The National
Union of Women's Suffrage Societies, Anna Martin described
her time at a women's settlement in a poor part of south-east
London. She observed how no chance visitor to the Lodge who
witnessed the gaiety of the members could ever guess at the
tragedies which lay behind. In her opinion, the poor were
temporarily able to throw off their anxieties in a way that not
only excited the admiration of more fortunate folk, but was also
worthy of a student of Eastern occultism. Masterman concurred
with these sentiments, arguing that life in the slums could not
be seen from the outside and then judged by some ideal standard;
rather, it should be viewed from the personal experience of its
inhabitants.

Despite the realism and attention to detail of many middle-class social investigators, their impressionistic observations – no matter how significant – remain just that. Their worth can be enhanced and their usefulness evaluated, however, by the second main source used in this study: the written evidence of working-class people themselves. This undoubtedly restores humanity to the urban poor and dispels any notions as to their bestial or sub-human nature. As Robert Roberts commented of Salford in *The Classic Slum*, perhaps the best and most perceptive working-class account of slum life: 'In spite of abounding poverty, it would be wrong to assume that the district lay slumped in despair. Much banter and good-natured teasing was to be heard. People laughed easily, whistled, sang on high days and jigged in the street – that great recreation room.'[4]

Other working-class autobiographies and quasi-autobiographies emphasise this fact that happiness was not absent in the slums, that misery and poverty had its humorous side too. In fact, they demonstrate that the urban poor snatched at jollity whenever the occasion arose precisely because of the terrible living conditions which took such a toll on their health and their lives. As Grace Foakes assured her readers in *My Part of The River*, whilst it may have seemed to many that the poor lived a miserable existence, this was not always the case.

As a source, working-class autobiographies are essential to complement and balance the comments of middle-class observers, and to enable the poor to speak for themselves. This does not mean that they should be used uncritically, a fault John Burnett is aware of avoiding. In writing down their memories, these autobiographers are engaging in an activity which sets them apart from the great majority of their class, with the consequence that they are not necessarily representative. This is particularly relevant to the urban poor; of those autobiographies which are written by working-class people, only a few are by members of this section or else are relevant to them. Robert Roberts acknowledged this in his own case when he wrote that, although he and his family lived in the slum, they were not of the slum. It must also be recognised that, whilst autobiographies are a direct record in which writers set down exactly what they wish to, they can as readily leave out what they want. Working-class autobiographers usually write about events in which they were involved many years previously, and the lapse in time can influence them to view their past in a jaundiced or overly sentimental way. This caveat can apply equally to another source used extensively in this study: that of oral evidence.

Over the last twenty years, increasing numbers of working-class people have been able to divulge their memories, unlock their backgrounds, release their feelings on their lives, and express their opinions on society, all as a result of the growth of oral history. Although their testimony may – like other forms of evidence – contain elements of bias, it has provided an invaluable means of supplementing the fundamental information which is to be found in working-class autobiographies. At the same time, the use of the interview technique has enabled historians to ask the crucial social and cultural questions not always addressed by the autobiographer. Whatever the qualifications as to their use, then, the importance of the written and spoken evidence of ordinary working-class people cannot be denied. Used in conjunction, they are indispensable both to our understanding of the way of life of the urban poor and to our awareness of how they saw themselves, their communities and society.

The other main source I have used in gathering the evidence required for this study is that provided by the Annual Reports of the Medical Officer of Health of Birmingham. These are vital regarding the statistics of life and death of slum life and, though prosaic, are as vivid, in many respects, as the writings of the social explorers. I have chosen Birmingham as the subject of this method of inquiry because, whilst this study represents a synthesis of much of the existing material on the lives of the women of the urban poor between 1880 and 1939, I have felt it necessary to focus on the women of one particular city as a case study, and to use original material in reference to them. Birmingham was an obvious choice for me, not only because it is my home town, but also because my oral evidence – originally assembled for my doctoral thesis, but now much expanded – relates to that city. It is also true that the importance of Birmingham as a centre of the working class is not reflected in historical research for the years from the late-Victorian period onwards. I hope that the evidence included in this study helps towards rectifying that situation.

Finally, a word about the period covered by this study. I have taken 1880 as my starting date because, although it is too distant to be of relevance to my oral evidence, the written evidence shows that, in many crucial respects, the 1880s were closer to the Edwardian era than they were to the mid-Victorian era. Important and wide-ranging changes had been occurring in English society over the preceding decades. England was, by 1880, a decidedly urban nation, and, in the decade it heralded, the way of life described in this book took hold in its industrial towns and cities. In the words of Eric Hobsbawm in *Industry and Empire*, the 1880s saw the completion of the process which saw the emergence of what is termed 'traditional' working-class life. During the same years, Charles Booth – pre-eminent amongst social explorers – carried out his investigations in London. His discoveries and those of other observers, coupled with the popularity of the novels of Walter Besant, ensured both an explosion of interest in the urban poor and the genesis of the East End into their symbolic home.

Although the First World War generated social changes which would ultimately transform English society, and in the process drastically affect working-class life, many required the catalyst of the Second World War to bring them to fruition. As a result, the inter-war period was a time in which the urban poor remained living, for the main part, in much the same way as had their parents and grandparents. That this was so came as a shock to the middle class, many of whom believed that the living standards and culture described by the late-Victorian social investigators had disappeared. The war-time evacuation of urban children disabused them of this fact. In the words of the Women's Group on Public Welfare who carried out a study between 1939 and 1942 entitled *Our Towns*, the effect of the evacuation 'was to flood the dark places with light and bring home to the national consciousness that the 'submerged tenth' described by Booth still exists in our towns like a hidden sore, poor, dirty and crude in its habits . . .'.[5]

In the wake of such revelations, and spurred on by a widely-felt need to improve the position of all of society's members irrespective of birth, the post-war years saw the development of the welfare state. Unfortunately, its inception and growth have failed to eradicate poverty. The urban poor did not disappear; they remain with us, but, shattered by social transformation and the post-war redevelopment, only vestiges of their former community life remain. It is for this reason that I have taken 1939 as the date at which my study ends. For it was then that the death knell was sounded for the hidden matriarchy of the urban poor, that most potent and significant element of their way of life.

Through the use of a variety of sources, I have sought to provide a view of the women of the urban poor that is truthful and relevant to towns and cities throughout England. I have also sought to bring them out of the shadows of the past and into the light of historical debate. In the process, I believe important lessons can be learned to help towards improving the welfare and living standards of the urban poor of today.

Chapter one

A hidden matriarchy

What a friend, what a pal, only now I can see,
How you dreamed and you planned all for me.
I never knew what a mother goes through,
There's nothing that you would not do.

Pal of my cradle days,
I needed you always.
Since I was a baby upon your knee,
You sacrificed everything for me.
I stole the gold from your hair,
I put the silver threads there.
I don't know any way I can ever repay,
Pal of my cradle days.

Dearest friend, oldest pal, it was me who caused you
Every heartache and sorrow you knew.
Your face so fair, now is crinkled with care,
I put every line that is there.

The words of this music-hall song, written in 1925, typify a genre
which abounded during the period 1880–1939 and which remains
popular still in many working men's clubs and public houses. It
is a style of song dedicated to the praising of the ideal working-
class mother, a woman whose first and last concern is the
welfare of her children and who sacrifices her life for their well-
being. Such songs can often be maudlin, but their excessive
sentimentality does reflect a potent and persuasive element in
working-class life, that of the almost fanatical devotion of a
mother to her children and their equally zealous devotion to
her. It is amongst the lower working class, the poor, that this
characteristic is at its most marked, a fact which enabled the

mothers of this section to exercise a power within their own small communities, which contrasts with the general lack of authority exercised by women of more prosperous classes during the period under review.

Any attempt to analyse and define the power any woman wielded during these years, let alone the mothers of the urban poor, ventures into an intellectual and, more importantly, emotional minefield. Personal, ideological and gender-based loyalties can all influence a writer's perception and opinion on this subject, as can the birth, upbringing and social background of that writer. It is certainly true – almost paradoxically so, given the fact of a female sovereign – that the years of Victoria's reign saw a withdrawal of women from most aspects of public life. The latter part of the nineteenth century witnessed the apparently complete triumph of a stridently patriarchal vision of society in which women played a definitely subordinate role to that of the dominant male. Consequently, the emphatic retreat of women – especially of married women – into the private sphere of the home in which they fulfilled the function of domestic manager would appear to have heralded the decline in the ability and potential of women to wield authority in society in general, a decline which was matched by a diminution in their control over their own lives. Yet, in many ways because of their poverty, lower-working-class mothers enhanced the status given them by the fact of their motherhood and succeeded, usually in a hidden way, in becoming arbiters of their own and their families' lives, as well as emerging as dominant influences within their communities. It must be pointed out that such communities were small, based on a street, a part of a street or, more rarely, a collection of streets. Nevertheless, whatever the size of the community, it is significant that women of the urban poor could defy society as a whole and assert their importance and essentiality to their own society and its culture.

In contradiction to this assertion, many surveys, investigations and commentaries tend to instil the view that the way of life of the lower working class was an extreme example of that which prevailed amongst the rest of society; that amongst the generally more conservative poor, total male dominance was the absolute norm. The belief was held – not without some justification – that women, especially wives, were little more than serfs, secondary in importance to the man and inferior and subservient to him in every way. Robert Roberts observed in his book, *Ragged Schooling*, that in Salford the women of the poor before the First World War generally called their husbands 'my boss' or 'my master'. Whilst this may have been an exaggerated and localised case, not only of female acquiescence in the accepted role of male superiority, but also of its open acknowledgement, attitudes like this had their echoes elsewhere in the country. In *Her People*, an autobiography set in the slums of Birmingham during the first years of this century, Kathleen Dayuss explained why, as a child, she felt that her mother did not bother about her daughters; it was because it was always: 'your dad must 'ave this' and 'your brother must 'ave the other'. Sons were generally more doted on by their mothers than were daughters, who had to fend for themselves, and this 'spoiling of the lads', the treating of them like lords, increased as they became wage-earners. A mother's daily tasks would often begin with the blacking of their boots, the laying out of their shaving gear and the pressing of their trousers. Many a working daughter must have wondered at such preferential treatment, given her equal importance to the family finances. The open favouring of the man and the acceptance of his superior position remained widespread and strong throughout the 1920s and 1930s but, in contrast to the earlier years of this book when women endured this relationship as natural, many younger women were beginning to resent if not actually challenge it: 'But when our Mom died he used to go mad. I was frightened of him. He used to say 'Come here! Stand there! Come and scratch my head!' One scratching his feet, one doing his head. More or less all men was pigs . . . It was all beer and sex then . . .'[6]

The stereotyped image of the drunken, lower working-class husband, mean with his money, callous in sex, uncaring of his wife's suffering, harsh to his children and ever ready to resort to violence, was too often matched in reality to become a parody. Such a husband was seen as a kind of absentee landlord, receiving what plenty there was in a slum household for his own selfish pleasure, draining his wife of money, affection and energy, and, most damning of all, unconcerned about the cost or the consequences so long as his own passions were sated. It was believed that these men knew only one way, that of the

overbearing ogre, and that they must be masters and accepted as
such in their own homes. This attitude was deeply ingrained, so
much so that even amongst husbands who were partners in a
more obviously egalitarian marriage it could still remain a
firmly-rooted belief. Doris Nield Chew's mother had worked as a
tailoress in a clothing factory in Crewe, and she and her
husband shared the same ideological and political beliefs, both
belonging to the Independent Labour Party and both active in
the union movement. Yet, in her book, *Ada Nield Chew: The
Life and Writings of a Working Woman*, which describes an
exceptional working-class woman who reached Socialist and
feminist conclusions about her life, Doris remembers that once,
whilst out cycling with her father, he expressed the opinion
that, after all, someone must be master. It is not surprising that
amongst the poor, generally more averse to change than other
sections of society, this belief was not muttered quietly but was
shouted out openly.

Meal-times, and especially tea-time, were perhaps the
occasions on which a man's importance was most clearly fêted
and his self-esteem most readily pandered to. In some households the father would eat on his own, the children too many or
too noisy or both, to sit with him. At breakfast, if there was any
bacon he would have it – with a morsel for a working son (but
not a working daughter); at tea-time – if finances allowed – the
monotonous fare of bread, with a choice of lard, margarine or
dripping to cover it, was varied by the addition of a relish or 'tit-
bit'. Delicacies such as brawn, corned beef, cheese, eggs, tripe,
pig's trotters, herrings, kippers or pickles would be his, with no
hint of complaint from wife, working daughter or children.
After all, was he not the breadwinner? Without his strength
being kept up, what would happen to the family if he could not
go to work? However, this law of the Medes and the Persians
that those who worked must always have the best patently did
not extend to the working women of the family. They had to
make do with as little food as possible, often doling out in tiny
portions to the children the already small pieces of relish they
might have received. Yet, whilst admitting that even in the most
liberal home the man was still better fed than his wife who might
also be working, was it true that all lower-working-class men
were tyrants, feared and often loathed, and, more importantly in

a way, were their wives, mothers and daughters as down-trodden, helpless and submissive as it might at first appear?

There were indeed many men of the urban poor who were domineering and who treated their wives in a feudatory manner – as, of course, did many men of other classes. It was a commonly-held belief throughout society as a whole, irrespective of status, that in the family God had assigned the first place to the man. Still, many men amongst the lower working class did not fit the mould of oppressor, bully and petty despot. A woman from Lambeth, in Mrs Pember-Reeves' study *Round About a Pound Week* (published in 1913), summed up the feeling of those who had caring and attentive husbands. She felt that her 'young man' was so good to her that it was as if something nice had happened each time he came in. As Mrs Pember-Reeves observed, this woman was obviously more articulate than most women, whose bald comment on their husbands that 'he was all right' might have meant as much as her more expansive one. In Salford, too, affectionate husbands and fathers were plentiful, to the extent that Roberts recalled in his other book, *The Classic Slum*, that one street was regarded derogatorily as 'Bloody Good Husband Street'. Roberts also expressed the opinion, which my own oral evidence from Birmingham tends to justify, that many men helped their wives in the house, so long as it was behind closed doors and workmates and drinking partners remained unaware of such assistance.

This 'hidden world' of many lower-working-class families, enclosed behind a façade of male dominance, separation of the sexes and female inferiority, is an issue to which I shall continually return in this book. Outwardly, the society of the urban poor conformed to its accepted image and indeed to the image it willingly projected. Inwardly, it was often at odds with that way of life. One middle-class observer before the First World War concurred with this view. M. E. Loane was a prolific writer on the poor and their culture and she believed that, whilst the ideal of fatherhood was less developed amongst the lower working class than was the ideal of motherhood, the men of this section were much libelled as fathers and that millions bore the blame that was only due to a few thousands. Furthermore, she felt that an increased knowledge of such men led to an increased admiration of their good humour and patience.

Even with regard to their children, these fathers might not necessarily be deficient in their responsibilities. Some took their children to the pictures as and when they could afford to, although each in turn, not all together as would an older daughter, and, of course, stopping off for a pint. Others even bathed them on a Saturday night and administered the weekly dose of brimstone and treacle or cod-liver oil. Like any other society, that of the urban poor cannot be seen in absolute terms: there were a great number of ignorant, insensitive and unkind husbands; there were equally those who embodied the reverse of these characteristics. More importantly, in between the two extremes lay the bulk of men whose characters – bafflingly to us today – were a hotchpotch of the praiseworthy and the despicable and who could exhibit both in a bemusing and apparently contradictory manner. An understanding of this fact leads to a truer awareness of the real nature of lower-working-class society and of the positions and roles of the women of the urban poor.

With all due recognition, however, of the provisos to be attached to the traditional picture of the men of the urban poor, it must be stated that, in the majority of families, it was the women who were the driving force. A family might survive without its father; it was rarer if it did so without its mother. Much of this book is concerned with married women and mothers. It is not that single women and daughters will be ignored or their importance will be diminished; they will not. Rather, it reflects a fact of lower-working-class life that, for most of their lives, most of the women of the urban poor were wives and mothers. The *Social Survey of Liverpool*, carried out between 1929 and 1932, reiterated the findings of previous surveys when it revealed that the proportion of adults who were married was very much higher amongst the working class than amongst other classes. This was partly an effect of the earlier age of marriage amongst the working class: in poorer inner Liverpool 29·5% of women aged twenty to twenty-four were married, compared with only twenty per cent in more prosperous outer Liverpool. This earlier age of marriage had an undoubted effect on the relative fertility rate of the various classes in English society. In 1905 the Medical Officer of Health for Birmingham, Dr Robertson, had observed that ninety-eight per cent of women in the twenty to twenty-four age group bore children, as opposed to 77·5% of women in the twenty-five to twenty-nine age group. Moreover, whilst lower-working-class women were more likely to be wives and mothers, as daughters they would, very often, have had to take on many of their parents' responsibilities and act as 'little mothers' to younger children.

Whilst the men of the urban poor were often maligned, so too were the women. The standardised image of the slum woman was of a person whose appearance and habits were commensurate with the miserable, squalid districts in which she lived. She was regarded as a foul-mouthed slut, over-fond of drink, careless as to her personal appearance and that of her home, ignorant of good principles in child-care and raising, and reliant on the pawn shop and the strap (credit) of the local corner shop to fill out the deficiencies caused by a squandering of housekeeping money. Jack London was amongst those who were pitiless in their condemnation of this antithesis of womanhood, of this negation of all that was feminine. The new race of the slums was the blighted progeny of 'rotten loins'; it was the diseased offspring of women who held 'carouse in every boozing ken, slatternly, unkempt, bleary eyed, and tousled, leering and gibbering, overspilling with foulness and corruption, and gone in debauch, sprawling across benches and bars, unspeakably repulsive, fearful to look upon'.[7]

Other commentators, whilst more restrained in their use of language, still adhered to the notion that the labourer's wife was a creature of limited intelligence and capacity. They affirmed that her only education should be aimed at inculcating in her the principles of sound household management, and of purging her of any desire to witness life outside the four walls of her home. Alexander Patterson in *Across the Bridges*, which described the Edwardian poor of Bermondsey, looked on lower-working-class mothers as mostly failures who were compelled to do as their mothers had done. He wrote of women who, by the time they were thirty-five, were frowsy and shapeless, and who had become dishevelled as their pride and confidence dissipated and their patience wore thin. Yet even Patterson was forced to acknowledge that a mother was the constant factor in the homes of the urban poor, that whilst others came and went she never disappeared.

Constancy was a factor which most mothers, whatever their social status, could possess. The mothers of the lower-working-class added to constancy a variety of other values which differentiated them, and which enabled many of them to belie the unwarranted title of failure as well as allowing them to escape from a subordinate role. These other values strengthened the position given them by the fact of their motherhood and gave them the potential to wield power within their own society, a potential usually denied to mothers who were more prosperous. Mothers of the urban poor embodied a multiplicity of roles which those mothers who were economically better-off could afford to delegate to others, or need not be involved in at all. An upper- or middle-class mother rarely went out to work; she might be involved in charitable activity, but that was voluntary and not paid employment and did not interfere with her duties as a housewife. Even with regard to her socially-acceptable role as domestic manager, she need not necessarily be personally included: a cook could be employed to cater for the family and to budget for the food bought; a housekeeper or charlady might be engaged to clean the house and to wash and iron the family's clothes; a nanny would often take over the responsibility of a young child, whilst an older one would be placed in a boarding-school, and, finally, a doctor could be called on in times of sickness whilst the nanny would nurse an ill child. In many respects, such married women – financially dependent on their husbands – were 'window dressing' to a man's pride, redundant in their position after bearing their children except in fulfilling the roles of dutiful wife and charming hostess. Similarly, amongst the upper working class it was 'not the done thing' for a married woman and mother to go out to work and, whilst she would clean the house, shop and cook herself, she might be affluent enough to pay a woman of the poor to wash and iron the family's clothes. These women too were seen as belonging to the house as much as did a man's material possessions.

In contrast, a mother of the urban poor was multi-functional in her nature. Over a period of years, and often all at the same time, she had to act as wife, mother, grandmother, housewife, cook, cleaner, household manager, nurse, defender of the family and helper to her neighbours in their times of trouble. She had to accomplish all that was asked of her – more, all that was expected of her – on less food, inferior nourishment and in worse health than her more economically secure sisters. Society decreed that lower-working-class mothers should perform the impossible: they should be competent cooks, providing the family with nourishing and healthy fare on a limited income; they ought to be provident household managers, experts in the raising of children; supportive wives as well as remaining scrupulously clean in self and home, whilst all the while forswearing any pleasure and refusing to succumb to any temptation to which the vicissitudes of slum life might sway them. If they failed in the objects set them by society then they were denigrated as useless, with little account taken of an irregular and inadequate income, insanitary housing conditions, or the needs of the human spirit. Moreover, if they went out to work to facilitate their task, to help translate impossibility into possibility by the infusion of additional income, then they were roundly condemned for neglecting the home for the survival of which they were, in fact, striving.

As an increasing amount of information concerning the lives led by the urban poor became available, more astute social observers began to realise that the mother was essential to the lower-working-class family in a way mothers belonging to other sections of society were not. Lady Bell – a perceptive commentator on the state of the Edwardian working class in Middlesbrough – felt in *At The Works* that it was precisely because of all the demands made on her and the variety of the roles which she had to fulfil, that the mother was the pivot of the working-class family. This was even more true of the mothers of the urban poor; it was they and not their husbands who were the key to both the future of their families and the condition of their partners. Lady Bell concluded that, happily, many such women carried their burden with a courage and a competence which was marvellous to the onlooker. Nearly forty years later and despite improvements in housing, sanitation and health care, the mothers of the lower working class who were described in Margery Spring Rice's study, *Working Class Wives*, were still carrying out the tasks that had been the essential prerequisites of motherhood for women of their class in the Edwardian era. It remained true that they required an unyielding maternal courage and that they accepted their lot with little complaint, indeed, often with much cleanliness and apparent satisfaction.

Anna Martin was a commentator who was particularly sensitive to the implications of lower-working-class motherhood. She extended Lady Bell's conclusions and, by so doing, dragged the mothers of the urban poor out of the wretched position of little influence many chose – and still choose – to see them in. At the same time, she stridently asserted their centrality to their families. She believed that amongst the poor classes there existed a marked superiority in the mental abilities of wives compared to those of their husbands. In her opinion, this superiority was induced by the ceaseless fight which women waged in the defence of their families against all the might of the industrial system. This battle led them to develop an alertness and an adaptability to which their men could not lay claim, their senses having become dulled and deadened as a result of laborious and uninspiring toil. The married working women who were described by Anna Martin were invariably mothers – or if not, soon would become so – and it is implicit in her argument that it was motherhood which stimulated the qualities she found so praiseworthy. Her pamphlet is of further unusual significance because in it she recognised the potentiality to wield power which was inherent in lower-working-class mothers. This accrued to them from the central place they occupied in their families; each mother knew perfectly well that the strength of her position was reliant on the physical dependence of husband and children upon her. In an article entitled 'Mastered for life: servant and wife in Victorian and Edwardian England', Leonore Davidoff made a persuasive argument for the belief that a wife's deference to the paternalistic status of her husband resulted in a subordination of a 'pervasive personal kind'. However, as Anna Martin recognised, the sense that they were the indispensable centre of their small worlds was the joy and consolation of the lives of mothers of the urban poor. These women might recognise that they lived in what was – at least on the surface – 'a man's world', but they did not necessarily accept that they were subservient to the male. This feeling is reflected in the oral evidence. As Elizabeth Roberts explained in *A Woman's Place. An Oral*

History of Working-Class Women 1890–1914, the oral testimony of women does not suggest that there was universal oppression of women within the working-class marriage. Indeed, in the great majority of marriages in her sample, the women extended significant power, not so much from legal right as from moral force. My own interviews imply that this contention is even more relevant to lower-working-class wives.

Devotion to her children was the catalyst which ensured the centrality of mothers of the urban poor and which enabled them to exercise authority. This power could only be wielded in tightly-knit, highly parochial and spatially limited communities. It is the overlooking of this fact that leads many writers to the conclusion that lower-working-class women lived only to service the needs of their menfolk and that they allowed their lives to be subsumed by the needs of their families. This view is enhanced because of the rare involvement of these women in political, ideological or trade-union movements which sought to better the living or working conditions of their sex or their class. Their lack of participation – or even interest – in such activities can lead to the feasible conclusion that they were weak and powerless. This would be erroneous. The poorest women did not have the time to consider the merits of organised co-operation, to debate a different social and political system, to demand a more comprehensive medical system or to seek an improved education for their children. Neither did they have the time to unite, to march, to protest, to write or to make their opinions heard. Poverty alone united the women of the urban poor. The fight against poverty was full-time, with little prospect of a break for leisure let alone involvement in socio-political activity. In the daily struggle to stem the tides of pauperism, the burning issues which excited the minds of more affluent women were not immediately relevant. The acceptance of this reality meant that, in this war of attrition, the allies of the women of the urban poor were not to be found in the accepted forms of working-class solidarity. Instead, as Elizabeth Roberts has termed it, they can be identified in a specifically female solidarity which was based on the extended family and the neighbourhood.

Survival of the family in a way which commanded the respect of others of their section was the aim which dominated the energies of most of the women of the urban poor. Struggle there certainly was in their lives to achieve this, and observers who disregard the success of many of them in attaining their goal demean their relevance to their particular society and the often powerful position they commanded within it. An emphasising of the obvious, namely the ascendancy of the male, does an injustice to lower-working-class women, whilst a continual desire to see them as merely the tools or dupes of their men belittles their determined efforts to overcome the often insuperable problems which beset them. A hidden matriarchy dominated the way of life of the urban poor of England. The fact that it was not open and readily acknowledged by many contemporaries and later writers, as well as the fact that it was not always recognised by the poor themselves, does not lessen its significance. Nor does it follow that those women who belonged to the matriarchy, by usually assenting to overt male supremacy were willing agents in submitting themselves to an inferior role. During the period covered by this book the urban poor lived in the midst of a society in which male supremacy was enshrined in the law, in religion and in social mores. Consequently, it is all the more remarkable that the women of this section defied society's dictates and attached to themselves not only importance but power.

It is by examining the relationship between mothers and their children, and particularly between mothers and daughters, that the concept of a hidden matriarchy is uncovered. More than the connections that existed between a husband and wife, parents and sons, or siblings, that between a mother and daughter was the most essential to the homogeneity of the extended family, to the interdependence of kin and hence to that most important manifestation of lower-working-class culture – loyalty to the street of residence and pride in the neighbourhood. Poor families inhered to their street, they came from it and it belonged to them whilst they also belonged to it. The streets in poor quarters became almost living entities, embodying the qualities which the poor themselves lauded: hardness, an ability to fight, and a character which was rough and ready and, above all, plain-spoken and down-to-earth. Outsiders amongst the working class did not talk of the residents and the street separately; rather they were one, a unity indivisible and frightening to those who did not belong. Thus it was that 'you didn't tangle with Studley Street', rather than 'you didn't tangle with Mr so-and-so from Studley Street' or a particular family or even the people of Studley Street. Equally, it was said that 'Summer Lane was the hardest and toughest in Birmingham but Garrison Lane was rough as well', rather than talking of the 'people of Summer Lane' or 'the inhabitants of Garrison Lane'. Whilst the street or lane (the poor nearly always lived in these which were older than the more modern roads) attracted to it many qualities which we might today term masculine, this was not necessarily so in the period under review. Amongst the poor, women who were strong, hard and rough and ready were praiseworthy and, furthermore, it was the women of the urban poor who engendered the loyalties which gave rise to the opinions held of the streets in which they lived, not that they did so consciously. Instead, it was a natural reaction to their importance to the way of life of the lower-working-class, as well as to their all-pervasive influence. In an analogy with birth, the poor spoke not of living in a certain neighbourhood or street but of 'coming out' of that street. This was not necessarily the street in which they were born but was the one in which they had been brought up. No matter where they might later live, the poor would evince a faithfulness to that street, a fidelity strengthened by its association in their early years with their mother, and in their later years because it was likely that their mother still lived there.

Residence amongst the urban poor was more usually matri-local than it was patrilocal; that is, married couples were more probably to be found living with or amongst the family of the wife than amongst that of the husband. This tendency was marked and has been observed in a number of studies, particularly those relating to the 1950s. Madeline Kerr's *The People of Ship Street* inquired into a very poor Liverpool neighbourhood. Of her sample of married couples, there were forty-four instances in which mother and daughter had lived, or still lived, in the same house. In a further thirty-two examples, the two women lived only five minutes' walk away from each other. In contrast, there were only eight cases of mother and married son living, or having lived, in the same house, whilst another eight lived within five minutes' walk of each other. In *Family and*

Kinship in East London, Young and Willmott's sample of forty-five married couples showed the same effect in Bethnal Green: it was found that, of twenty-one couples who were living with their parents, no less than fifteen lived with the parents of the wife.

From this evidence relating to the 1950s, can it be extrapolated that mothers and daughters were as close, spatially and emotionally, in the years 1880–1939? There are no specific studies which might prove or disprove the assertion that they were. The evidence from a variety of sources is, however, suggestive. Gwendolen Freeman noted in her book that one daughter, like so many in the district with which the book is concerned (Summer Lane), brought her husband to the house of her parents. Furthermore, the writer believed that this woman, again like so many others, had no choice, that such an occurrence was inevitable given the way of life of the poor. Hints also occur as to the strength of the mother-daughter relationship in the earlier years of this study. In 1881 a local Birmingham newspaper (*The Balsall Heath Times*) reported the case of a man charged with abandoning his wife and children so that the local authority had to pay for their keep in the workhouse. In court the husband declared that he would take care of them and maintain them so long as the authorities kept 'the old lady', his mother-in-law, away from their home! A woman from Sparkbrook in Birmingham remembers how her father coped with a similar situation at the turn of the century: feeling that his wife was too close to her family because they lived in the same quarter as the couple, he moved the two of them and their young children away. Like many lower-working-class men, however, he eventually had to admit defeat. His children were later to be raised in that same neighbourhood amongst his wife's family and they showed a strong loyalty to their maternal grandmother.

Indeed, oral evidence is firm in emphasising the strength of the matrilocal tendency amongst the urban poor. Between 1914 and 1934 one woman (in an example relevant to many others) raised a family of twelve in a poor part of Aston in Birmingham. On marriage, the three eldest daughters took up residence – as a matter of course – in the same small street (Whitehouse Street) as their mother. Between them a further seventeen children were brought up there, whilst for much of this period – the 1930s and 1940s – the five younger daughters of the family remained single and at home. In turn on her marriage, one of these was very unwillingly housed on a distant and newly-built council estate. She returned constantly to her mother's home – often to sleep the night or, if going back to the estate, taking a favourite niece with her as company. As this woman remarked with hindsight, moving away was not even contemplated. It was taken for granted that a daughter's home would be established near that of her mother. This latter point, too, is very important; the home always belonged to the mother, not the father. In all lower-working-class families a visit home was to 'our Mom's' not to 'our Dad's'. A. P. Jasper, in *A Hoxton Childhood* (set in London before the First World War), remembered how his father returned home from work one day to find that the family had – in the meantime – moved to another house. It was only through information given by neighbours that the so-called head of the household found out his new address. As his son commented, the move had nothing to do with 'the old man'; rather it was the decision of the mother of the family.

What engendered such closeness between mothers and daughters? In the case of Ship Street, the families were living in large houses which had formerly belonged to the middle class and, as a result, there was more room for married daughters. The living conditions in Bethnal Green were more cramped, so it was more likely for a younger daughter to remain at home on marriage than it was for an elder daughter, who had probably married whilst her younger brothers and sisters still remained at home. Yet the question remains as to why, all things being equal, the home of the wife's parents should be preferred? As Young and Willmott point out, mother and daughter were used to each other, they were aware of each other's traits and characteristics and were less likely to be rivals for a stove, a sink and even a man than would be mother-in-law and daughter-in-law. There remain, however, even more compelling reasons. In Birmingham's poor areas large families living in tiny, two-bedroomed, back-to-back houses often made the lodging of married daughters impossible. Yet these showed a strong desire to live as close to their mother as possible. Of course, a mother who was well-established and widely respected in a district would be ideally placed to recommend a suitable couple to the landlord or agent of a vacant house nearby. More than this was involved in the relationship though. A mother was a sought-after helper and comforter in childbirth as well as in the days after birth. She could be readily called on to mind children if a mother returned to work, whilst being a constant fount of wisdom and advice with regard to the raising of children and their health. Indeed, it was a matter of much comment by health visitors that lower-working-class mothers, especially those who had large families, were very conservative in their methods of bringing up infants and preferred the advice of their mothers and grandmothers to that of the professionals.

It is important to be aware, however, that not only daughters wished to live near their mothers, so too did sons in many instances. This tendency too was matrilocal, as the sons wanted to live near their mothers rather than their fathers, as shown in Young and Willmott's survey. Very often the desires of both partners in respect of residence could be satisfied, given the higher rate of 'local marriages' amongst the poor; the urban poor were more likely to marry someone from the same street or quarter than were the upper working class or middle and upper classes. Thus, very quickly, a lower-working-class street could become the scene of a network of both closely and distantly related families. In Studley Street, Sparkbrook – a short street of just two hundred yards' length with eighty-one houses - the Educational Census Books for the years 1908 to 1910 indicate that there were five families sharing the surname of Warwick; three with those of Jones and Stokes, and two each with those of Moore, Reeves, Fletcher, Chambers, Harris, Hyde, Beedon, Bashford, Parton and Fawkes. In nearly all cases, families with the same names were close relatives, the heads of household being brothers, fathers, sons or nephews. Intermarriage between the families strengthened these ties, as one resident of the street graphically described:

Nack Carey ... he was related to the Prestons ... Alf Chinn married Ada Wheldon, then he married her daughter afterwards Maisy Derrick. It was the different families that was intermarried. There was Rounds' ... he had about fourteen or fifteen kids.
There was another Rounds which was related to them lived next door ... The old lady Carey which was related to Nack Carey ...Next

door was some distant relation to me . . . Granny Gloster.
Lenny Hinchley was a kid when his parents died and he was adopted by
the Reeves' . . . because . . . Mrs Reeves was a Hinchley . . .
As I say, three quarters of the street was like a clan . . . [8]

Between 1906 and 1914 fourteen marriages took place at
the parish church of the district in which at least one of
the partners was resident in Studley Street: in ten cases
both partners came from the street (three of them living next
door to each other); in a further three the union was with a
partner from elsewhere in Sparkbrook, and in only one instance
did one partner live outside the neighbourhood, in this case
coming from the adjoining area of Balsall Heath. This lower-
working-class quarter of Birmingham was not unique in its
endogamous nature, and in particular Hugh McLeod has
revealed the way in which endogamy was relevant to working-
class communities in London at the turn of the century. In
Class and Religion in the Late Victorian City, he compared
the marriage patterns of four parishes in the capital: in St
Clement's, Notting Hill, unskilled manual labourers were a
majority; in St Andrew's, Bethnal Green, skilled manual
workers were the largest element, whilst St Mary's, Lewisham
was a middle-class parish and St John's, Paddington was
wealthy. Within these parishes he identified various neighbourhoods. These were defined as areas which were less than
half a mile square and which were neither crossed by a railway,
waterway or main road, nor were they broken up by a park or a
belt of factories. His findings from a much larger sample
emphasise the significance of those for the Studley Street
locality. Whilst in both the Bethnal Green and Notting Hill
parishes the majority of men married a woman from their own
neighbourhood, in the latter 'poorer' area the figure was eighty-
two per cent compared with a lower sixty-five per cent for the
more upper-working-class district of the two. In the much more
prosperous and different class-based St Mary's and St John's
parishes, the figures relating to 'neighbourhood' marriages
were twenty-five per cent and nearly twenty per cent respect-
ively. There seems little doubt, in the light of the preceding
evidence, that the poorer the neighbourhood, the more likely it
was to be characterised by the strength of its inter-family
relationships.

The urban poor, then, were very parochial in their way of life, more so than were other sections of society. It was this parochialism which strengthened the position of mothers, grandmothers and older sisters. Women appeared more permanent in their attachment to the street than did men – especially adult men – and this fact, together with the coalescence of blood ties into community, facilitated the rise of a matriarchy. The female triumvirate of grandmother, mother and daughter was dominant over its male counterpart and was bolstered by the respect the great majority of sons had for their mothers. This respect permeated every aspect of the community life of the lower working class, and it was as forcefully evident in those regarded by society as incorrigible. Alf was the anti-hero of Clarence Rook's commentary on the hooligans of Lambeth but, whilst he had many faults and was an imperfect creature, he was always a good son to his mother. A crucial effect of both endogamy and the esteem in which sons held their mothers was that, although it was commonly believed that once married a son was lost to his wife's family, in reality this was not necessarily so. Furthermore, the bachelor son, refusing to marry whilst his mother remained alive, was a familiar figure in the neighbourhoods of the urban poor. This son would not, however, usurp the authority of his mother or even of a dominant sister. A man might be the breadwinner and thus be regarded as the head of the family, but it was a woman who was its focus. From amongst the women of the family a matriarch would appear, someone around whom the family revolved and upon whom its members relied for advice and often leadership – although this might not be obvious out of respect for a man's accepted role. It would be she whom the family came to see, and it was her home which was the meeting-place of the extended family.

In most lower-working-class streets matriarchs were a familiar and ever-present sight, often huddled in easily recognisable groups. Helen Forrester was of the opinion that during the 1930s the poor of Liverpool lived in highly matriarchal communities. Her socially important autobiography, *Twopence To Cross The Mersey*, related the traumatic experiences of a middle-class family forced by bankruptcy to live in the slums. In it she depicted ferocious grandmothers and wagging mothers as reigning so supreme in the poor quarters of the city that men had hardly a toehold in the home. Robert Roberts saw these matriarchs as a powerful inner ring of grandmothers who dominated the poor areas of Salford so long as they maintained their own home. Certainly grandmothers did make up a greater portion of the matriarchs in similar neighbourhoods throughout England. Their age and experience of life, a veteran's instinct and knowledge as to how best to wage war against the effects of poverty all combined with a usually greater length of residence in a street compared with younger women to ensure that many grandmothers became promoted into matriarchs. The uniform of these women, too, tended to induce respect. Kathleen Dayuss evoked their image when she described her own grandmother as always dressed in a full-length, black taffeta frock, black boots, a battered black woollen shawl and a black lace bonnet with ribbons. Her character was also in keeping with the mould of many matriarchs; she was stubborn, very defiant and independent and she possessed a fierce temper.

Matriarchal grandmothers could have a softer side, and this was at its most visible in their relationship with children. Maternal grandmothers in particular provided a welcome and trustworthy substitute for a working mother in the care of her infants. Indeed, the phrase 'granny-reared' was often applied to these children as well as to those who were actually raised by a grandmother. The oral evidence from Birmingham suggests several reasons for this latter phenomenon, a common one being the size of the family of a daughter or even daughter-in-law. One or more children from a large family would frequently go and live in their grandmother's home and be brought up by her. This occurrence was made easier by the parochialism of the urban poor in that grandmother and daughter most probably lived in the same street or neighbourhood. Less formal arrangements were also familiar. For example, various grandchildren might sleep at their grandmother's as the mood took them, or grandmothers might feed their grandchildren who would return home to sleep. Another regular reason for 'granny-rearing' was the death of a mother, unfortunately not an uncommon happening in the slums. In such instances many fathers were grateful to relinquish their parental responsibilities to their mothers-in-law or mothers. One more fairly frequent cause of this circumstance is most indicative of the communal self-help of the urban poor and the divergence of their culture from that of the rest of society. Amongst upper-working-class, as well as middle- and upper-class, families, an illegitimate baby was a social embarrassment, even a disaster, which had to be disposed of either through adoption or by making an outcast of the mother. This was not normally the effect produced on a lower-working-class family; instead the child would be raised believing its grandmother to be its mother, and its natural mother to be its sister. The successful maintenance of this fiction depended on the tacit support of the local community; one illegitimate child of a long-established family in the Studley Street locality learned the details of her birth in her late teenage years only as a result of the unmeant indiscretions of a very old woman. Catherine Cookson, the author of *Our Kate. An Autobiography*, also grew up believing her grandmother to be her mother and, though her playmates in East Jarrow disabused her of this fact when she was only seven, she continued to call her grandmother 'Ma' and her grandfather 'Da'. In a very real sense, then, most youngsters of the urban poor had two mothers, with the result that the influence older women had on them cannot be underestimated. A powerful bond was forged between the young and the old, and the growth of a feeling of mutual devotion could only enhance the prestige of grandmothers.

Not all grandmothers could successfully turn themselves into matriarchs. They might be shy, retiring or even weak, and one trait required more than any by a woman in this position was strength of character. It was for this reason that a daughter might supersede a mother and become the matriarchal figure of a family. Eldest daughters in particular were apt to do this. Their consequence to a large family was great and, as a result, they too had the potential to dominate that family. Responsibility was thrust onto them from an early age, turning them into 'little old women'. From as young as eight or nine years old they became the nursemaids of younger children and the valued and much-needed support of their harassed and over-worked mothers. Walter Allen vividly represented their type when he described Lizzie, Billy Ashted's big sister, in his novel *All In A Lifetime*. Because she was the oldest and a girl, she had always had a special relationship with her siblings, acting as a second mother, 'a miniature woman'. She had washed her brothers and sisters, cared for them, rocked them to sleep, scolded them, protected them, fought for them and ruled them with a rod of iron. In Ashted's opinion, life without her would have been impossible, and it seemed as if she had no existence apart from the family. Patterson assented to this sentiment, describing how girls of tender age, as they set off on 'running' errands for their mothers, would also be wheeling prams full of children whilst others trailed behind.

The eldest daughter of a poor Birmingham family of twelve recalled how her responsibilities increased even further when her mother was taken into hospital for a serious operation in the 1920s:

I'd got a stop with all the other kids. Could a been thirteen. And our kids used to cry for our Mom . . . I nearly killed our Winnie when our Mom was in 'orspital. I fed her that bleedin' much I nearly killed her. Farley's and Nestles milk. I used to feed her every ten minutes. I kept thinking her wanted to be fed. Anyway Sundays our old mon used to get all the dinner prepared . . . and he'd go the 'orspital, have a few pints on the way. We'd have our dinner and I'd have to clean up and wash up. And I promised 'em one Sunday,
'If you all be good, I'll wash you and put you clean and we'll go and see our Mom'.
And I took 'em and I thought The General was the 'orspital our Mom was in. I said
'It's a long walk and they won't let us in 'cus we're not old enough.'
Get's 'em to The General and stands 'em on The Law Court steps. And I said
'Stand on her, you'll see our Mom'
And they used to have the balconies and you'd have the beds on the balconies if you was getting better. And I said
'There's our Mom!'[9]

Eldest daughters undoubtedly led harder lives than their younger siblings. They became accustomed to denying themselves for their sakes and were constantly alert to the demands of duty. Yet most did not resent the role of protector and provider which the accident of birth had inflicted on them. Instead they delighted in their position, relishing the stature it gave them and welcoming the dependence of younger brothers and sisters on them. It was this latter especially, which was strengthened by a more patient and good-natured attitude towards their charges than was often evinced by mothers, that enabled an eldest daughter to assume the mantle of matriarch more easily than other women. This more than compensated for an education interrupted by frequent absences from school caused by a need to look after infants or sick children whilst their mothers were at work.

Roberts mentioned one or two families whose mothers had become cyphers. Worn out by too much child-bearing or broken by chronic disease, they had lost all authority, powers, privileges and duties, relinquishing them to an eldest daughter. He believed that the rise in status of these young women was bought at a price: they were expected to remain unmarried and they became the drudges and unpaid servants of their families. However, this was normally not the result if the daughter married, nor need it be if she did not. In Raphael Samuel's *East End Underworld: Chapters in the Life of Arthur Harding*, the central character strongly emphasised how his unmarried eldest sister, 'Mighty', took the mother's part in their household. His earliest recollections were of her taking him with her on errands for their mother and of her taking time off from school to look after him. As she grew older she became the economic mainstay of the family as well as its emotional one, providing the means by which all its members were able to get on in life. 'Mighty' Harding could easily have acted as a model for thousands of other eldest daughters as she bought treats for Arthur and paid for him to go to the theatre, giving him the only pleasures he knew as a youngster. In the case of A. P. Jasper's family, the eldest daughter Mary was one of a minority who was unwilling to assume a position which entailed so much self-sacrifice and thus she abandoned her role. This was willingly taken up, though, by Jo, the Jasper family's second eldest daughter. She became her mother's right hand and staunch ally, defying her father on many occasions and refusing to acknowledge his right to have their mother at his beck and call. Jasper, like most younger brothers, adored his sister, an emotion which augmented the importance of women in general in poor areas.

Young women like 'Mighty' Harding and Jo Jasper were undoubtedly the stuff of which matriarchs were made. As such, as Roberts expressed it, they would become the guardians of the group consciousness, the repositories of intimate knowledge of each family and the means by which information that might be

useful to their families or neighbours would be passed on.
Indeed, helping others in her community was a major attribute
of a matriarch. This quality was not confined to her; poverty
ensured that conflict – ever ready to break out in the slums – was
always balanced by co-operation in the characters of the poor. It
was an almost unquestionable duty of all slum dwellers to help
those of their neighbours who were in need. This might take the
form of washing for a woman who was sick, or of minding her
infants, or of giving precious coal to a family with young
children that lacked it. As a Birmingham woman remembered of
her poverty-stricken childhood in the 1920s:

You wouldn't go hungry not if next door had got any bread . . . You'd
get a piece, if it was only a piece of bleedin' stale bread. There was some
very hungry times. We was poor as bleedin' church mice, poorer than
that . . . Now, Mrs C was a rough and ready woman, her dyed her hair
all colours. Her used to come out and her med her face up like a harlot,
but that woman'd got a bleedin' heart of gold, I can tell you mate. Now,
the lads in the street used to play outside her house . . . and all of a
sudden one'd be 'ungry. They thought nothing of dashing into Mrs. C's
house.
   'Can we have a piece, Mrs C?'
   'Oh, I ain't got no bread. Go and arsk Mrs Tuckett to send me a loaf
and half a pound of margarine.'
They used to fetch that loaf in her house and her used to cut that loaf up
for them kids.[10]

This particular woman was not a matriarch, and some women in
her street looked down on her because of her personal appearance and the condition of her home. Yet she adhered as strongly
as they to the belief that the poor should help each other, as did a
woman who was a definite outcast in the same small community.
Though married, she was a 'semi-prostitute', but her status as a
pariah was mitigated because at times she used her earnings to
pay the rent of needy neighbours.

   It is with justification, then, that C. F. G. Masterman claimed
that in all the world there were no other people who helped
each other in the manner of the urban poor, nor were there any
who showed greater kindness to those in trouble. Lady Bell
concurred with this sentiment, as did Madeline Kerr, who
commented on the neighbourliness of the poor in times of
trouble. The tight-knit nature of their communities ensured
that neighbours always seemed to know when help was needed,

as Helen Forrester explained to her socially-aloof mother in *Liverpool Miss*, the sequel to her autobiography. 'Survival networks: women's neighbourhood sharing' forms part of a title of an article by Ellen Ross which looks at this form of communal assistance, and the phrase admirably sums up its ramifications. This kind of help was not institutionalised, nor was it formalised. Rather it varied according to need and circumstance. In her other book, *Where There's Life*, Kathleen Dayuss recounted how, when widowed with four children at the age of twenty-eight, a collection made by her neighbours helped her to pay for her husband's funeral. Money was obviously a scarce commodity in the slums and neighbourly help usually took other, more readily available forms, the most common of which was the lending of food or belongings. A neighbour of Catherine Cookson's regularly borrowed her family's bread knife and her mother's boots, whilst a grandmother in the Studley Street quarter habitually lent her own washing to desperate neighbours so that they might pawn it. Ellen Ross noted how a Mrs Barnes, who sold cooked sheep's heads and pigs' feet in Hoxton, often gave a free meal to needy neighbours, or else distributed amongst them any food she had left over at the end of the day, and Elizabeth Roberts reported that this type of help was also to be found in the North-West. Indeed, amongst many of the urban poor, alongside a spirit of 'penny capitalism' there existed this communistic attitude to property.

Ellen Ross identified another telling aspect of this collective self-help when she discussed the prevalence of informal adoption amongst the lower working class. She instanced the case of a mother of four who lived in a very poor South London neighbourhood which had a reputation for criminality. When a widow who lived nearby was sent to prison, this woman took in her two children, reasoning that it was only 'neighbourly-like' for her to do so. This type of informal adoption was especially common for short periods; when Grace Foakes' mother was taken into hospital for three weeks her children lodged with neighbours, as did those of Kathleen Dayuss when she went into hospital to have another baby. However, permanent fostering was not uncommon, although this kind of arrangement was not a formal one and was often entered into with little or no discussion on the part of the families concerned. Gwendolen

Freeman gave the example of a 'simple' child who was taken in by a slightly more prosperous family than his own who lived in the same court. The same thing happened to the younger daughter of a Birmingham family of twelve, and her experience showed that unhappiness could ensue from arrangements of informal adoption if they were entered into between families of dissimilar economic status:

Momma Rose had got a shop down the round and Mom had to go in for a serious operation when I was little . . . I was crying all the while and Momma Rose had me. And, 'course, that caused a lot of trouble in our lives, 'cus Mom couldn't do enough to repay her. And 'course they had a cooked meat shop and Mom was forever down there cooking and cleaning . . . Her 'ad me and then I decided to go home while I was still little. Then her had Rosie. Then her had Junie. Her had Rosie quite a few years 'cus Rosie knew when her was well orf . . . but her only lived a few doors away . . . I don't know whether Mom, with having so many of us, thought they'd 'ave a better life.[11]

Such instances of fostering were rarer than those between relatives. As the previous discussion referring to granny-rearing showed, relatives were normally the first recourse of parents who felt the need to allow their children to be fostered, with aunts, especially if they had a small family, also favoured.

Impoverished parents, who allowed any of their children to live with relatives, or neighbours, only marginally better-off than they, were plainly unable to pay for the keep of their offspring. It was the recognition of this fact which prompted Gwendolen Freeman to declare that, in the practice of informal adoption, the urban poor manifested a blithe kindness of which middle-class people would have been incapable. This was most obvious with regard to orphans who were seen as a particular responsibility of the extended family. As Anna Martin found, despite their own poverty, strenuous efforts were made by relatives to keep these children out of the dreaded workhouse. One woman she knew took in an orphaned nephew aged three. She accepted, because of the straitened circumstances of her immediate family, that she would be obliged to let the Guardians have him when he grew older. Yet, as long as she could find a 'bite for his mouth', she was determined to keep him with her and not send him to a place where there was no woman to love him. Several orphans in the Studley Street neighbourhood were brought up by aunts for the same reason, but it is interesting that a number of orphans who had no other relatives in the locality were raised by neighbours. Catherine Cookson noted an instance of this in the North-East when she quoted the case of the Regan family whose children were distributed amongst their neighbours after their mother died, and Jerry White also mentions this kind of occurrence, again in relation to a very poor neighbourhood, in *The Worst Street in North London. Campbell Bunk, Islington between the Wars.* These examples provide further support for Ellen Ross's argument that neighbours and the neighbourhood acted as auxiliary parents. At the same time, they run counter to the belief expressed by Michael Anderson in *Family Structure in Nineteenth Century Lancashire* that the working class employed a 'calculative orientation towards kin'. The great majority of instances of informal adoption could not produce a monetary gain for the foster parents, neither could any other form of neighbourhood sharing. It is true that, at some time or other, every poor family would need the assistance of neighbours and relatives to help them through a difficult period, but most forms of co-operation were patently not the result of selfishness. Help was not a commodity such as money which could be loaned out and called in as a debt when circumstances rendered it expedient. Communal sharing and self-help were selfless acts tendered, in most cases, with little thought of profit or reward. Cynics might disagree, but I concur with Elizabeth Roberts in having little doubt that the working class were more than capable of acting altruistically, unselfishly and lovingly.

If the urban poor assisted each other because they believed it right to do so, then matriarchs gave help more regularly and consistently than most, not just because it was right but because it was their duty. Some matriarchs specialised in a specific skill necessary to ameliorate the lives of their neighbours; others were adept at all. In Birmingham these women were often distinguished by the addition of one of a number of prefixes to their names which were indicative of the status and respect in which they were held by their communities. Thus, in the Studley Street quarter there were to be found, from the 1890s to the 1940s, Mother Minton, Old Mother Fletcher, Granny Carey, Old Girl Garbutt, Old Lady Snow, and others to whom these titles could apply. Their maternal position was not restricted to their own families; it became extended to embrace each and every family in the street. These women were not unique to Birmingham. The oral evidence contained in *Bristol As We Remember It* mentions that in the 1920s and 1930s there lived in Salisbury Street a Granny Hodges, and it would seem that most lower-working-class neighbourhoods could boast their matriarchs and 'wise women'.

The duties of these women were many and varied. As unofficial midwives they were present at births as valued and much-trusted advisers and helpers and, in the years when most women were confined at home and state-registered midwives lived outside the neighbourhood, they were an essential and reassuring presence. In *Old Wives' Tales, Their History, Remedies and Spells*, Mary Chamberlain remembered with pride that her great grandmother was the 'angel of Alsace Street'. An 'old wife' or 'handywoman', her personal attendance was much sought after and appreciated at the births in her neighbourhood. Entry into the ranks of unofficial midwives was achieved not by examination or affirmation by the 'educated'. Rather the test that had to be passed was dependent on the more immediately relevant one of a woman's experience of life. Mary Chamberlain's great grandmother qualified through having served an apprenticeship distinguished by bearing sixteen children, and the unqualified local woman who delivered Albert Goodman in Stoke in 1890 was in demand for similar reasons. In *Destiny Obscure: Autobiographies of Childhood, Education and Family from the 1820s to the 1920s*, edited by John Burnett, he accounted for her popularity in terms of her motherly nature and her reputation for successful deliveries. As with Old Lady Snow of Studley Street, neither of these women could gain financially from their duties, nor would they expect to. More important to them was the respect in which they were held by their neighbours.

With the increasing prevalence of 'hospital' births, the services of unofficial midwives were rendered obsolescent, although in poorer areas they lingered on into the post-war years, as Madeline Kerr found in Liverpool. Progress, redevelopment and a different social climate had the same effect on another responsibility of 'old wives'. In a superficially incongruous but really quite harmonious duality of roles, unofficial midwives often 'doubled' as 'layers-out'; they washed and dressed the bodies of neighbours or relatives who had died. If the death had taken place at home and the deceased was Church of England – and, as opposed to nonconformist sects, this denomination seemed strong amongst the urban poor – it was the custom for the body to lie in its own house for seven days before its burial. In these circumstances, the first call of the bereaved was on the local woman or women who 'laid out'. Their duty was to wash and dress the body, in the process tying a handkerchief around the head and under the chin and placing pennies over the eyes. In the same manner as unofficial midwives made no charge for their services, neither did layers-out; as one interviewed by Elizabeth Roberts said, she performed this 'good deed' as a 'good neighbour'. Once laid out, an undertaker would then be called in and the body placed in an open coffin so that those who wished could view it and pay their respects. All the while ordinary family life was carried on, although on the night before the funeral close family and friends of the deceased would sit around the coffin and perhaps have a drink. In many respects this vigil corresponded to the Irish wakes, although at these jollity was much more evident, a Birmingham woman remembering that at the wake of the mother of an Irish friend of hers the body was stood up in its coffin whilst the merriment went on. Festive-making was not, however, absent from the funerals of the urban English poor; it was reserved for after the burial, not before it. A family was seen as deficient in its duties to the deceased, and to its neighbours, if at their home they did not provide a 'spread' for the mourners after the funeral. As Robert Roberts drily remarked, boiled ham on the bone was eaten so often at funerals that to be 'buried with 'am' became a comic's cliché. Whilst the family would purchase the food for the 'funeral feast', it often devolved upon one or two local 'mothers' – commonly the community's layers-out – to prepare it. These 'helpers' would guard over the 'spread' whilst the funeral took place and also help to distribute it. Of course, a bonus of this duty was that the helpers would share in the 'feast', although most would have done so anyway, given their positions within the local community.

Matriarchs had other responsibilities with regard to death apart from laying-out. One Birmingham 'mother' rented a house with two rooms downstairs. This type was uncommon in the city's poorer districts and was esteemed at the time of a death because the deceased could be laid out with more decorum in a little-used front room than it could in a living room or bedroom. It was a boon, then, for less fortunate neighbours that the Birmingham woman allowed them to lay out their dead in her front room – at no cost, of course. Another important duty was to collect money from neighbours of the deceased so that a wreath or wreaths from 'the street' could be sent to the funeral. Catherine Cookson recalled her annoyance when she realised that as much as two pounds would be collected and spent on flowers whilst the bereaved – perhaps a widow – did not know from where her next penny was coming. Yet the wreaths from neighbours were a solemn communal gesture which affirmed the 'belonging' of the deceased to the community. Kathleen Dayuss was made starkly aware of this as a girl when no wreath was sent on the occasion of the death of a female Jewish money-lender who had lately moved into her area. A collection was not made for this woman precisely because 'she wasn't one of us'.

Sickness also found neighbours seeking the help of 'mothers', this time those who were knowledgeable in 'folk medicine'. These women were not comparable to the rural 'old wives' who sold salves, ointments and charms – although they too may have been extant in a vestigial fashion in some urban areas. Rather, they were usually older women who could advise a simple and readily available palliative for minor complaints, such as a bread poultice to draw out a boil, or the soaking of feet in urine to cure a person of chilblains. This kind of home doctoring – not unusually available as a prepared medicine at the local chemist or herbalist – was, as Mary Chamberlain observed, often a matter of common-sense. Other women might be sought in times of emergency, not because of their supposed knowledge of medicine but because they provided a calm and authoritative voice at a time of emergency and were respected for that quality.

Strength of character was particularly relevant to those women who were matriarchs and who did not necessarily possess a skill useful to their communities. These matriarchs were distinguished by their forceful and dominant personalities and within their neighbourhoods were widely recognised as leaders. In Birmingham, back-to-back houses were usually terraced in small courts which were known colloquially as 'yards' and, as a woman from the very poor and ill-famed Garrison Lane quarter of the city remembered, every yard seemed to have its 'gaffer' (boss) who would always be a woman. Kathleen Dayuss's mother was of this type. Physically and emotionally strong, often hard, always independent, these women were at times resented because of their domineering way. Yet they remained admired and respected because they 'got things done' and could be relied upon as organisers. Inevitably, one of these matriarchs was 'the someone', as described by Catherine Cookson, who would 'get up a trip'. In her community, that 'someone' was usually Old Mrs Powers; in Garrison Lane it was a woman bookmaker, and in the Studley Street locality it was Old Lady Waldron. All three were prominent in their communities not just on account of their drive and organisational abilities, but also because they were trusted. It was their duty to collect money each week off those who were interested in going on a particular trip and they had to be relied upon not to disappear with 'the club money'. This kind of outing was a specifically 'women's' affair; the annual 'charabanc' (coach) outing arranged by Old Lady Waldron, for example, was for the benefit of the neighbourhood's married women. In the 1930s she was, however, the instigator of children's outings to Rhyl as well as the driving force behind large-scale street parties. Indeed, the oral evidence suggests that trips were very much events which occurred in highly settled neighbourhoods after 1919 and – at least in Birmingham – that they were very much reliant on the financial assistance of local bookmakers to make them feasible.

Perhaps the most important function carried out by women who were 'gaffers' was as authorities in the self-regulation and self-control of the communities of the urban poor. This is a vital point to be aware of. In neighbourhoods where the police were so often regarded as outsiders, it was the poor who governed themselves socially. Anna Martin recognised that amongst the masses there existed many curious traces of the era before written laws and organised legal systems. She believed that the lower working class adhered to a kind of common law – she knew no other way of describing it. In her informed opinion, it was this which largely regulated their relation to each other in a way quite independent of, and sometimes in spite of, the law of the land. In a more down-to-earth manner, a man from the Studley Street neighbourhood expressed the same view in relation to his own Edwardian childhood:

They was rough and ready but they was disciplined, you know. They didn't stand no nonsense which was only right and proper... if anybody got a bit bossy and the rest of the neighbours thought they was putting on an act, you know, trying to be funny about it, there'd be somebody to pull 'em to order. They'd soon be straightened out. They'd let 'em see they didn't want anybody bossing 'em around. You'd got to toe the line. There was more democracy amongst them in their rough and ready way than there is today.[12]

The 'somebody who'd bring 'em to order' was inevitably a physically strong matriarch, an acknowledged and unchallenged leader of the community. In fact, the man just quoted could remember an occasion when his mother punched a neighbour and knocked her down because she was 'dictating'.

As will be discussed later, women who fought were not rare in the slums of England's towns and cities, and instances of individual retaliation against those who offended them in some way were not unusual. Examples of communal retribution of a physical kind against those who contravened the moral codes of the urban poor are harder to find. Catherine Cookson believed that, in general, people turned a blind eye in these cases. If a mother was cruel to her children, they might stop speaking to her or else they might talk about her, but they rarely did anything. Incest, too, could damn a household but, as Robert Roberts recalled, a strict public silence saved the miscreants from the law. The oral evidence, too, would imply that the disgust and punishment of the community against those who offended against its moral sensibility usually manifested itself in ostracisation or in talk. Neither of these was necessarily a weak and ineffectual response; it would be an unusual man or woman who could live for long amidst those by whom they were shunned, ignored and censured. The talk of neighbours was an expressive and often effective means of social control; that of matriarchs was even more so. 'Rough justice' was, however, an option available to the community, but it was rare and likely to be enforced only against those who so blatantly and un-ashamedly contravened the moral standards of the urban poor that their behaviour could no longer be ignored or left to the condemnation of whispered conversation. Catherine Cookson wrote of one woman whom the moralists nearly ran out of their midst because she was trying to take another's husband. A woman from Aston in Birmingham recalled a more violent episode in the 1930s. A mother of four killed herself when her husband, a well-known womaniser, left her. Galvanised to carry out retributive justice, older local women gathered outside the public house where he was drinking. It was their intention to wait until he left and then attack him with shopping bags laden with potatoes and swedes. It transpired that these weapons did not need to be used. In the pub's yard the offender was so badly beaten up by the neighbourhood's 'hard man' that he ended up in hospital. On his discharge, he was ostracised and forced to leave the locality. This kind of occurrence was uncommon, although the implied threat of violence against transgressors was not, but the usual response of matriarchs to wrong-doers was to enact their displeasure through their conversation.

According to Robert Roberts, one of the most vital forms of social control which matriarchs had was that they presided in judgement over the public behaviour of both children and young teenagers, reporting back to mothers the peccadilloes of the younger generation so that they might be punished. In *The Queen's Poor: Life as they Find it in Town and Country*, M.E. Loane endorsed and extended the implications of Roberts' opinion, although in an oblique way. She stated that few well-to-do people realised how much self-control and selflessness were necessary before peaceable times could be had in crowded quarters. I would argue that, in neighbourhoods where self-control successfully ensured a certain harmony which made life bearable for the poor, it was as a result of the strength of the matriarchy and their beneficial influence on all the members of their communities irrespective of age. The respect with which the matriarchs were regarded, the esteem in which their opinions were held, and the fear of the ubiquitous nature of their reprimands combined to give them a moral power in their neighbourhoods which no men could match. Of course, this kind of hold over the daily life of their neighbours could be abused;

talk could degenerate into gossip; conversation could deterior-
ate into scandalmongering. A woman who grew up in Studley
Street in the 1940s remembered that, for her, the street's clique
of older women always seemed to find something wrong with
everyone else. Nevertheless, I believe that the matriarchs were
an essential feature of the neighbourhoods of the urban poor.
Without them, slum life would have been much more difficult to
survive and could easily have become intolerable. In the words
of Melanie Tebbut, the author of the excellent *Making Ends
Meet. Pawnbroking and Working-Class Credit*, elderly women
were the linchpin of the street network, they had a hand in
everything that happened from birth to death and they belonged
to a 'hidden society'. This hidden matriarchy, then, both
balanced and superseded the open patriarchy of the slums and
was able to do so because motherhood was the source of its
power.

Chapter two

The power of mothers

The devotion of most lower-working-class children to their mothers is exhibited not only in the tendency of daughters, and to a lesser extent sons, to prefer to live near that parent, but it also emerges clearly in the great majority of autobiographies written by those who had been born into poor households. A. P. Jasper dedicated his book to his mother and to all the mothers of the time of his childhood and youth (the first years of this century). In his opinion, his mother was the most wonderful woman in the world and he found it difficult to describe adequately the love that she gave to her children. Happiness, he believed, had always been denied to his 'poor mother', a woman whose efforts and energies had staved off starvation from her children and had prevented them from drifting into criminality. This is a theme common to many similar autobiographies; the belief that the mother of a poor household was the only safe harbour in the midst of the uncaring and often cruel sea which was society. A child's confidence in his or her mother's unswerving support when beset by problems was rarely misplaced. Alexander Patterson observed that most lower-working-class mothers knew little of their children's actions, yet, whilst ignorant of the facts which might lead one of them into trouble, would be prepared to leap like unreasonable tigresses to their defence. A popular saying amongst the urban poor, that a mother would always remain a child's best friend, no matter how deep the relationships that might be formed in adult life, adds further credence to Patterson's opinion.

Helen Bosanquet, in *Rich and Poor*, regarded this enthusiastic and unstinting loyalty which lower-working-class mothers had for their children as a 'terrible devotion' which could not hope to produce a dutiful or affectionate son, except by a miracle. Yet much evidence, oral and written, would seem to suggest that miracles occurred regularly amongst the urban poor. Patterson noted that when a son went away from his family he would send many postcards back to his native town, but only one to his home and that to his mother. A Birmingham man remembered how in 1931 at the age of sixteen he joined the army, purely because his mother's continual child-bearing and her necessary attention to the needs of younger siblings was relegating him in importance to his mother and precluded her from devoting herself solely to him. The two remained in constant touch by letter, however, and when on leave the son would always take his mother out for a treat, but her alone, not his father or any of his brothers or sisters. Even the terminology used by the poor towards their mothers was a further indication of children's devotion: a wife was the 'old woman', a mother 'the old lady', a title bestowed upon her, as Gwendolen Freeman observed, with a hint of respect as well as of affection. It was the reciprocal relationship of devotion between mother and children which gave to these women the potential to transform themselves into matriarchs and thus command respect and exercise power. Not all mothers could translate potentiality into reality. The central figure of Grace Foakes's home was her mother, yet her centrality did not enable her to gain any authority, because her husband dominated the whole family and did not allow his wife a say in anything. Alice Foley, born ten years earlier than Grace Foakes in 1891, loved her mother passionately but in her book too, entitled *A Bolton Childhood*, her father dominated the family until his children entered adulthood. In contrast, Dolly Scannel, in *Mother Knew Best: An East End Childhood*, described an overtly patriarchal household which was covertly but strongly dominated by her mother. The author depicted her father as lord and master in his own home but immediately asked the question 'or was he?'. She then went on to wonder if, in fact, her father was only a paper tiger invented by her mother for some subtle reason of her own.

Specifically, it was the ubiquitous nature of a mother's self-denial which ensured her children's devotion; it was certainly not through an open demonstration of her love through touch, speech or a general tenderness. Clementina Black, in *Married Women's Work*, published in 1915, was of the opinion that parental affection was the ruling passion of the women of the poor, and certainly many mothers were kindly like Alice Foley's, or the mother of Mrs Layton from Bethnal Green who wrote 'Memoirs of seventy years' in *Life As We Have Known It*, published by the Women's Co-operative Guild in 1931. Yet a kindly mother need not usually be demonstrative and many women must have resembled Dolly Scannel's mother who, whilst she was a woman who knew what it was to care and feel sympathy, did not know how to express it. Amongst the poor, as with other sections of society between 1880 and 1939, a premium was not placed on an open exhibition of love between members of a family. In general they too shrank from an obvious manifestation of their love for each other. In *My Mother's Story*, an account of slum life in Birmingham during the 1930s and 1940s, Wyn Heywood could not remember a single sign or gesture of affection which any one of her family had ever shown her. Not one of them had ever put their arms around her or had even taken her hand. Indeed, she could recall the occasion she broke down and cried as a result of a nun from her convent school giving her a peck on the cheek before she returned home. The autobiography of Margaret Perry is another which is included in John Burnett's collection relating to childhood and family. In it she recollected that the members of her Nottinghamshire community did not use words like 'love' and 'kiss'; like other forms of endearment, they seemed to stick in their throats. In fact, amongst her class and in her society the word 'duck', being 'Nottinghamese', was the only acceptable term. Blandishments seemed redundant amongst the lower working class, so much so that their use seemed incongruent, as David Christie Murray bore out in *A Capful o' Nails*, his novel about the nailmakers of the Black Country which was published in 1896. His narrator, the young Jack Salter, brought to mind the way in which his father's use of the term 'my pretty wench' to his mother aroused her consternation. Her husband was surprised at her response, feeling that because she 'hadn't many' fond words she would have appreciated them.

Most lower-working-class mothers must have become inured against showing tenderness, their affection an early casualty in the cruel war of attrition raged by poverty. Dolly Skinner, the central character in *A Walk Down Summer Lane*, John Douglas's semi-autobiographical novel of Birmingham slum life during the 1930s, would seem to epitomise this type of mother. She is portrayed as a tough, no-nonsense character, ever-willing to work and fight for her children, but completely unable to give vent to her feelings towards them even though she desperately wished to. As Douglas observed, expressions of compassion and sentimentality had not been part of Dolly's social education; instead of telling her children that she loved them, she expressed her affection in gruff-mannered ways in which her love was disguised as a kind of rough coarseness. In a hackneyed but correct truth, life amongst the urban poor was hard and it induced a hardness of spirit amongst mothers as much as it did amongst anyone else. Sympathy was a feeling a mother of the poor could not afford to express to a child – no matter how much she might long to – as, by becoming accustomed to it, a child was left defenceless against the trials which would beset it in slum life. The lesson had to be learnt early, as one Birmingham man remembered on the occasion of his starting school at the age of four. He recalled being led off snivelling to his class where the teacher 'sweetened' him with a ride on the rocking-horse. Despite this, he continued to cry but, on looking to his maternal protector for sympathy, all he received was the curt reproach: 'Stop ya blarting and behave yourself!'

In some mothers this hardness was not just skin-deep; it transferred itself into a feeling almost of indifference towards their children, other than that they owed them a duty to work for them whilst they were young, solely by virtue of the fact that they had physically borne them. Maternal compassion and love seemed to be squeezed out of these women, leaving behind a kernel almost devoid of emotion. Kathleen Woodward was born in 1896 and grew up in Bermondsey, the setting of the fictional *Jipping Street*, the title of her autobiography. As Carolyn Steedman writes in the introduction to the Virago edition of this book, Woodward was bound to her mother not by love but by a fierce sense of resentment and debt. Her mother was described as a woman fearless and without hope. Flinty, enduring, strong and proud, she was a granite-like person who did not ask and who did not receive. She sweated and laboured for her children without stint or thought, but remained utterly oblivious to any need they might cherish for sympathy in their sorrows or support in their strivings. Simply, she was unaware of anything beyond the needs of her children's bodies. George Acorn, in *One of The Multitude* published in 1911, represented his mother in much the same vein. He was grateful to his mother for her 'quite, quite' heroic struggles to supply her family's physical needs, yet he wished that to her strength of purpose could have been added some spiritual sympathy, some ray of tender love. If this had happened he would have responded with generous affection, his mother becoming so much to him. Acorn was left supposing that life to his mother had been an iron mould in which all plastic sympathies had been compressed.

Both George Acorn and Kathleen Woodward not only regretted their mothers' lack of love, but resented the fact. Still, they remained grateful to them for their physical efforts on their behalf, as did Kathleen Dayuss who was sure that her mother did not love her and who at times felt that she hated her parent. Nevertheless, Dayuss remembers feeling lucky to have a mother of any kind, as some children in her neighbourhood had no mother at all. Mothers such as hers could often only show affection when a child was seriously ill. Acorn remembered how his mother nursed his younger brother who later died; how she tried to still his fitful cries with strange, sweet, soothing invocations. This unfolding of the great, loving maternal instinct in a previously apparently unfeeling woman came as a revelation to her eldest son. It is evident that, whilst there were many mothers such as his in the slums, insensitive to or simply unable to respond to their children's emotional needs, nearly all mothers of the urban poor were united by an adherence to an ideal of motherhood in which self-sacrifice was the dominant emotion. A mother need not give of herself spiritually, so long as she did so physically. A bad mother was not one who might be stern, strict and sterile emotionally, but rather was one who neglected her children's bodily needs. In this light, the mothers of both Kathleen Woodward and George Acorn were good mothers, a fact which the latter's landlady reminded him of when he complained to her of his parent's lack of affection. It is, therefore, through the provision for the bodily wants of their children that the self-denial of lower-working-class mothers is most evident.

During 1908, as a result of an approach by the Home Office, the City of Birmingham Health Department carried out an investigation into *The Industrial Employment of Married Women and Infantile Mortality*. The survey concentrated on the poverty-stricken central wards of St George's and St Stephen's, where in 1896 sixty-three per cent of the houses had been of the badly built, inadequately ventilated and insanitary back-to-back type and were between sixty and one hundred years old. In his report for 1909, Dr Robertson, the Medical Officer of Health for Birmingham, declared that mothers of the urban poor:

... live more exacting and self-denying lives than probably any other group in the community. I have personal knowledge and have the testimony of many reliable workers, that what food comes into the house is given to the children or the husband, while they themselves go on from day to day in a state of semi-starvation.

The life of a mother among the poorer classes is always a strenuous one if the family is large, but when hunger is added, and particularly when such a woman is an expectant or nursing mother, the condition is a particularly distressing one.[13]

Two years later Dr Duncan, who was in charge of the ongoing investigation, reported that she had paid many unexpected visits to the homes of these mothers and found that many of them were having only tea with bread and lard for breakfast and supper. In some cases the diet was even poorer. During much of her married life Wyn Heywood, though working, existed solely on bread and margarine for dinner and on potatoes and swedes for tea. At one stage, in the 1930s, she suffered from fainting spells which a doctor, called in by her employer after she collapsed at work, diagnosed as the results of malnutrition. A mother did not eat with her family, she snatched a bite here and there. She was server and provider for all and it was her job to see that everyone except herself received their fair share. This applied as much to an expectant mother as to any, as the second correspondent in *Maternity Letters from Working Women* (published in 1915) explained. This was supported by the Reverend T. J. Bass – vicar of the parish of St Laurence, arguably Birmingham's poorest and most deprived – who quoted a Church Army nurse in *Everyday in Blackest Birmingham: Facts Not Fiction* (published in 1898) as knowing of cases where mothers had gone for three days without food after their confinements.

A mother's self-denial was invariably associated with the provision of food for her family, particularly her children. The Reverend Bass knew of many 'heart-rending' cases of young widows pawning the very clothes off their backs in order to obtain a few scanty coppers with which to supply the immediate wants of their starving little ones. Rose Gamble in *Chelsea Child*, set in the 1920s, compared her mother to a street sparrow, foraging to feed and protect her offspring with neither thought nor energy for anything else. The abnegation of lower-working-class mothers ensured, as in the case of Rose Gamble and her brothers and sisters, the importance of that parent and the consequent dwarfing in significance of the father, whilst the devotion of the children to her created an indestructible family unit based on the centrality and essentiality of the mother. As Alexander Patterson argued, throughout her life a mother of the urban poor had given life at the risk of her own; she had loved her children sincerely, if not wisely, in her own inexpressive way; she had fed them first; scrubbed while they played; washed while they slept; tidied up after them, and was ever by their side at the crises of their lives. It was she who drew the strings together and made a home. With her gone, the family would often fall away because she was the centre, the most permanent and important member of the family.

In another of her works, *The Family*, Helen Bosanquet argued that amongst all the classes of English society – except at the extremes of wealth and poverty where in the former the mother could abandon the home for pleasure and in the latter for paid employment – a wife and mother was based at home. It was her duty to manage and spend the family income and care for the home, whilst it was the duty of the husband and adult children to provide that income. In reality, what distinguished all mothers of the poor, whether they worked or not, was their total command of the family finances in every respect, except for that money retained by a husband for his own pleasure. An unwritten law decreed that all working children gave all of their wages to their mother, who in turn decided the amount she would return to them as pocket money. This sum increased with age and income but the principle remained immutable, determined by her children's loyalty and trust in her, as well as by her intrinsic importance.

Her children's earnings not only supplemented the household budget but bestowed on her a certain independence from her husband which could be advanced if she herself worked. Whereas more financially secure wives, including those of the upper working class, were reliant generally on the wallet of the husband, it was the purse of a mother which was the common fund amongst the families of the poor. She it was who paid the rent, who bought the clothes, who purchased the food and who applied for credit at the local corner shop. It was she who conducted all financial negotiations and it was upon her generalship that the family relied to supply it with a meal.

M. E. Loane was amongst the few commentators on the lower working class who realised the considerable influence that this financial control gave to the mothers of the poor. With a keen appreciation of the real centre of power in the households of these families, she declared that the custom of leaving the management to the wife was so deeply rooted that the children spoke of the family income as belonging entirely to their mother. She was of the opinion that fathers were regarded by their children as plainly inferior to mothers in authority, in knowledge of right and wrong and, above all, in manners. Far from lower-working-class wives being under the subjection of their husbands, she felt that the 'bare idea' of a father being equal to a mother in rank and authority never entered the head of any 'cottage child' under sixteen. Indeed, fathers were usually regarded as a mother's eldest child and disobedience in him was a more heinous crime than in them because, 'he'd ought to know better than not to do what mother says'. Nevertheless, a wife was reliant, to a greater or lesser extent, for funds from her husband to swell the housekeeping money, particularly if her children were not in full-time employment. The women of Lambeth described in Mrs Pember-Reeves's study generally lived just above the poverty line. On the whole they seemed to expect judgement to be passed on their husbands according to the amount of housekeeping money that was allowed them. In most cases it was felt that if they handed over less than twenty shillings a week to their wives, explanations were required. Yet most mothers of the urban poor often had to manage on a considerably smaller sum given them by their husbands. The father of George Acorn gave his mother eighteen shillings a week when they first married and never increased the amount. When work fell slack, his mother suffered the loss of wages; when work was plentiful and overtime the order of the day, his father would have time off, spending the extra on drink. Money matters never troubled Acorn's father in the least; he took all the meals, so anxiously provided for, without the slightest thought or consideration, often trying to borrow some cash from the few coppers of housekeeping that remained.

A man such as this was not exceptional, nor was he necessarily condemned for his insensitivity and selfishness. Rather this was the accepted pattern of life amongst the poor. As Mrs Layton stated, despite leaving the responsibility of the family to their wives, men such as these could be good husbands and fathers up to a point. However, in the case of nearly all fathers, the money that they kept back for beer, tobacco, betting, or whatever, remained theirs solely and was not to be regarded as part of the pool of money for the family. As the daughter of a Birmingham man who was out of work for most of the 1920s vividly remembered:

Our Dad kept his whack for his booze and if our Mom hadn't got any money and he'd got money he wouldn't give her more, he'd go and booze it. She med do the best as she could. Our Mom's sent me – if her'd got a copper or two – her's sent me to Mason's on Ladypool Road – where they sell the bacon and eggs and everythink – for two pennyworth of bits of bacon. We used to come home with a big parcel of it and a pen'orth of speced tomatoes from Bliss'. That used to be our dinner. They had to cook it over the open fire. That was your lot. Might have a piece of bread and margarine – never butter – or a piece of bread and lard, piece of bread and dripping.[14]

Another woman from the same city recounted how, on one occasion at the turn of the century, her grandmother had made a meal for her large family on the threepence given her by her husband, all that was left after he had squandered the rest on drink and gambling. The woman cooked a stew consisting of two pennyworth of pieces of meat and a pennyworth of mixed vegetables which, temporarily at least, satisfied the hunger of her children. Wyn Heywood's father too was a gambler and her mother a heavy drinker when she had money, yet regularly during the 1930s a meal was provided on fourpence, always consisting of three pennyworth of breast of lamb and a pennyworth of swedes and potatoes.

Most men did assent to the notion that they should provide their wives with the larger part of their wages each week, from which the whole of the family should receive the benefit. Yet a minority of men expected their wives to manage with little or no contribution to the housekeeping from their earnings. A woman from Paddington remembered with bitterness that, during much of the 1920s, her father regularly gave her mother a farthing a week wages, expecting his wife to pay for everything out of her own earnings. As a result, even though she loved to go to the pictures she was unable to afford to treat herself. A. P. Jasper could not recall his mother ever having a proper week's money off his father, six or seven shillings a week being the most she ever received. Her husband reasoned that he need not give his wife regular housekeeping because she was always able to earn a few shillings with her sewing machine, and this should provide for her family. Very often the young Jasper would return home from school to find that there was nothing to eat in the house until food could be purchased with the sale of a bonnet his mother had made. Alice Foley's father worked fitfully between bouts of drinking and gambling and often disappeared to stump around the country agitating for his passion, home rule for Ireland. Her family too relied on her mother plodding gamely on and supporting them out of her wash-tub earnings. The worst disaster that could happen to any lower-working-class family, whether or not the father was generous, was the illness or incapacity to manage of the wife. It was essential that she keep on going somehow to prevent the disorganisation and dis-comfort of all. In consequence, many women were like Bessie Clive, an acquaintance of Gwendolen Freeman; they forgot how to sleep.

It was only when a wife's strength was totally sapped and illness struck so severely that she was removed from the home, or she was absent for some other reason, that some men became aware of the privations undergone by their families and particularly by their wives. Mrs Pember-Reeves recited the case of a Lambeth husband who helped with the housework and cooking, with the result that their home was one of the most spotless seen by the author's visitor. Yet, when a charity organisation paid for his wife to have a holiday at the sea-side and he was left to care for himself and five children without her guidance, it emerged that this man, more con-siderate and aware than most, allowed the weekly consumption of margarine to rise from 1s 6d to 3s 6d. This was because he allowed margarine all round on the same scale as he had always been used to it himself. Additionally, the weekly gas bill rose to 2s 3d, when no baking had been done, as opposed to 2s when his wife was at home and there had been baking. During the second week of his wife's absence, savings had to be made and thus no coal, matches, soap or cleaning materials were bought, whilst the father was further obliged to put every penny of his own pocket money into the general fund over the two weeks his wife was away. The eldest daughter of the Birming-ham family of twelve clearly, and distastefully, brought to mind her father's culinary ability when her mother lay seriously ill in hospital: the family lived on stew; stew for Sunday, stew for every day, stew for breakfast as well if there was any left.

In spite of the salutary lessons which were taught a few men, most carried on in the accepted manner, blithely unaware of their wives' sufferings and lack of comfort and, even if they were, expecting them to carry on doggedly. They were like Joe Simmons, a character in *Love on the Dole*, Walter Greenwood's intuitive novel of Manchester slum life during the 1920s. He endowed money with the qualities of elastic when it was in his wife's hands, and accused her of incompetence when she failed to produce the miracle of all their wants. Ada Nield Chew recounted, with relish at his discomfort and disappointment at his reaction, the story of a man who shared the same attitude and who was challenged by his wife to better her performance in managing the household. For a month he took charge of the housekeeping money of twenty-two shillings a week (he was in the habit of keeping another four shillings for himself). He found that he was quite unable to cope on this sum. Yet, at the end of the month when control of the family finances reverted to his partner, he steadfastly refused to increase her allowance. His conscience was untroubled by his inaction, soothed by the argument that he had married his wife to manage and manage she must.

Middle-class observers were not interested, however, in the failure of the occasional husband to manage a household. Instead, they were deeply concerned by the apparent inability of large numbers of wives to make do on what appeared to them the adequate sum provided for a family's needs by a 'typical' labourer's income. The wives of the urban poor were condemned as ignorant, thriftless, and careless, and Helen Bosanquet was a perfect example of those who denigrated them. She chose to see them as women who scrambled along from day to day, taking what came, never asking for more, and spending wastefully what was given them grudgingly by their husbands. Dr Robertson was in full accord with her sentiments. In 1914 he declared that many daughters of the urban poor were growing into womanhood without a proper experience in the things which went to make a healthy home. He believed his remarks especially pertinent with regard to the catering and cooking for a household, which was, in many cases, as bad as it could be. Lower-working-class mothers were regularly portrayed as women who could not cook, sew or wash; who were unsuccessful in managing their husbands and keeping them out of the public house; who were ineffective at raising their children and inadequate in the nursing of their babies, and who were also ignorant of all questions of health-care. If this image is a correct one, then what power a woman might accrue from her control of the family finances would dissipate as she squandered her money and so lost any respect her children might have had for her. Yet if it is not true, then it is obviously through a skilful manipulation of the meagre funds at her disposal that a mother of the urban poor could consolidate and augment her authority.

A contributor to *The Moseley and Kings Heath Journal*, which circulated in a very affluent suburb of Birmingham, wrestled in 1895 with the problem of how a lady of gentle birth could live on an income of forty-five pounds a year. In his calculations the writer made a daily allowance of sixpence for meat, twopence for bread and a penny for milk; a weekly allowance of 1s 6d for washing and two shillings for the rent of a house; an allowance for vegetables, butter, sugar and tea, and not forgetting a yearly one of four pounds for the wages of a servant. The correspondent concluded that it was possible for a lady to live on under thirty-five pounds a year. He could only pity one unfortunate enough to have to try the experiment, however, given the allowances made; the inability of engaging a first-class general servant on the sum mentioned, and also considering that no figure was allowed for broken crockery. His hypothetical exercise was, of course, dependent on a regular income, as were most of those of other educated observers who calculated the potential of lower-working-class mothers to provide a healthy, nutritious and balanced diet for their families without falling into debt. That most were so patently unable to, only made more credible the belief that they were improvident and extravagant. Little account was taken of irregular earnings, the mean of which were usually the lot of the unskilled poor who were forced into casual and seasonal work and under-employment if they were to avoid complete unemployment. Over a year, a family of six, seven, eight, and not uncommonly more, had to survive on the skills of a mother with eighteen shillings a week or less at her disposal, or ten pounds a year more than that allowed for a single lady of gentle birth. Furthermore, much of what was taken for granted in the calculations for her survival would have been superfluous or indeed unnecessarily wasteful in the opinion of the poor: employing a servant and a woman to do the washing were both absurd and unnecessary when a wife could accomplish the manifold tasks of both, and the purchase of meat and butter every day was an unaffordable luxury, whilst the after-thought of no allowance for broken crockery would not have been considered by the poor.

The constant expenses of the lower working class were more mundane and realistic: rent, burial insurance, coal and light, cleaning materials, clothing, and food that filled a hungry stomach rather than tempted it. It was impossible for the poor to meet the demands made by all of these on the money a wife had at her disposal, as proved by Mrs Pember-Reeves in Lambeth. There, most men were in regular employment and gave their wives around a pound a week for housekeeping (hence the title of her book). The local Board of Guardians allowed a foster mother four shillings a week for food in the case of a child boarded out; the author allowed a typical family of six, two shillings a week each for parents as well as for children. There then remained a meagre eight shillings, the bulk of which was swallowed up by rent of six to seven shillings a week, leaving a pittance to pay for gas, coal, insurance, clothes and cleaning materials. In the study edited by Clementina Black the case was quoted of a London woman, Mrs A., whose family income was 31s 3d a week. After deducting 6s 6d for rent, a sum of 4s 1½d remained to provide for each member of the family. The writer was left to wonder incredulously how provision could be made for a family on such a figure, which left not a farthing for recreation or enabled any comfort, luxury or leisure and which also disbarred mental energy and the raising of healthy children. If finances were so tight amongst the better-paid and regularly-employed of the working class, how much more straitened were they for the poor? Furthermore, the problems of the lower working class were compounded by the relative expense of living in the slums. Again, as Mrs Pember-Reeves highlighted in an attempt to dismiss the fallacy that it was cheaper to live in poor neighbourhoods, it was the less-well-off of society – those who could least afford it – who contributed a disproportionate amount of their earnings on rent, rates and taxes. A well-off, middle-class man paid one-eighth of his income on these items; a comfortable middle-class man, one-sixth, and a better-off working-class man on a wage of twenty-four shillings, one-third. To exacerbate this discrepancy, most housing for the lower working class did not have water laid on; nor did it have coal cellarage to enable the poor to purchase fuel more cheaply in bulk and, lastly, the light and ventilation of their accommodation were inferior, so that illness amongst the occupiers was more commonplace than amongst the more affluent of society.

How then did a mother of the urban poor manage on an often uncertain income? The most important factor was the character of the woman herself; her ability to manage on insufficient housekeeping and still maintain the family in independence, without drifting into destitution and total reliance on charity or the local authorities in the form of the parish. Many women were like George Acorn's mother, adept at eking out their funds by one device or another. She may have been an illiterate, but she was a woman with a good headpiece who was remarkably sharp in repartee and was quick in reckoning. As Lady Bell observed, everything depended upon the wife; the husband's

steadiness and capacity to earn were not more important than
the wife's administration of the earnings. In fact, it was
usually this latter which was pre-eminent, given the inability
of the poor to determine a regular figure for the housekeeping.
Anna Martin stridently declared that even the Labour leaders
failed to realise how entirely the burden of the family amongst
the lower grades of workers fell on the wives. The man gave
what he could afford or what he considered adequate and
the wife had to make it suffice. In a stinging rebuke to
those of the middle class who castigated the wives of the
poor, Ada Nield Chew declared of her charlady, Mrs Turpin,
that every day she solved a problem, by reason of her experience
of life and her heroic devotion to duty, which had hitherto
baffled civilised governments. In addition, she brought up
her children on a sum which housekeepers on a large scale,
with the advantages of buying their food in bulk, found totally
inadequate for such results as she produced. The writer of
the article on the district of Leek and Macclesfield, in the
work edited by Clementina Black, could only marvel at how
the mothers of the poor kept their children and houses so
well on so small an income and with so little time left them
from outside work. Helen Forrester's middle-class parents
contrasted unfavourably in her young mind with the Hicks
family who lived in the basement of their dwelling in the
slums. Forrester's parents had received no training in the
management of a family of seven or of a domestic budget and
they continued to smoke cigarettes and hire taxis they could
not afford, whilst her father fell swiftly into debt by borrowing
from the local fish and chip shop owner. Mrs Hicks had also
received no formal training – except perhaps at school during
cookery and hygiene lessons – yet she was an excellent
housekeeper who understood the nutritional value of cheap
foods like herrings and lentils, and who was aware that brown
bread was better for the diet than white bread. Poverty had
induced in her the alertness of mind of which Anna Martin had
spoken, and it was such women who led Peter N. Stearns to the
deserving conviction that, with regard to the quality of their
housekeeping, women among the very poor in Britain were in
many ways better adjusted than the average working-class
woman.

It was in connection with their cooking abilities that wives of the urban poor were most often chastised for their ignorance. In reality, it was on this issue that many exhibited an ingenuity and adaptability that was more worthy of praise than it was scorn. Food was the most elastic of the items on their budget, and it was the amount spent on this which was regularly reduced if their income deteriorated beyond what was an already financially tight situation. Seebohm Rowntree illustrated the predicament in which many wives found themselves. One of the families in his study belonged to his Class B. That is, they were of that group where the income for a moderate family of between two and four children was more than eighteen shillings and less than twenty-one shillings a week. In effect, this family straddled the poverty line. The wife was reported as an exceptionally clever and economical housekeeper, but every extra for the family was bought out of the money set aside for the purchase of food. This, even at its normal level, was 4s 5d a week less than the sum which was required to provide them with the same diet as was supplied to able-bodied paupers in the York work-house. Mrs Pember Reeves quoted a governmental report with respect to the Poor Law in which the recommended diet for a child over two and under eight years was as follows: for breakfast, five ounces of bread and half a pint of fresh milk; for dinner, one and a half ounces of roast beef, four ounces of potatoes or other vegetables, and six ounces of fresh fruit pudding, and for supper, four ounces of seed cake and half a pint of cocoa, half of which was to be milk. It was impossible for a wife with twenty shillings a week or less to spend on managing the household to provide such fare for a husband, let alone herself or her children. Consequently, mothers sought to assuage the appetites of their families with relatively cheap, starchy but filling foods. Given their limited finances, they could hardly do otherwise. Yet it was for this that they were so often condemned because it was felt that such a diet was unexciting, unscientific and was lacking in nutritional value.

The investigators who researched the social survey of Liverpool compared working-class expenditure on food in that city beween 1929 and 1932 with that calculated by the Sumner Committee in 1914. In spite of the real rise in wages which had occurred, the lapse of time, and the political and financial upheavals which had taken place between the two surveys, both were surprisingly similar in their findings. Spending on bread and flour was exactly the same, at nineteen per cent of the total household income; expenditure on meat, fish, etc., was $31\frac{1}{2}\%$ in 1914 and dropped only one per cent in the later survey; the amount spent on tea rose by $\frac{1}{2}\%$ to seven per cent; that on potatoes and vegetables by one per cent to eight per cent, and the most significant rise was the $4\frac{1}{2}\%$ on milk to $10\frac{1}{2}\%$. A slight drop in the amount spent on cheese was recorded, whilst that on sugar fell $\frac{1}{2}\%$ to four per cent. The similarity in expenditure between the two surveys is striking; even more so are comparisons of studies in which the diet of the poor was examined.

Many of these are included in John Burnett's informative study, *Plenty and Want. A Social History of Diet in England from 1815 to the Present Day*. During the 1860s, Dr Edward Smith carried out investigations into diet on behalf of the Privy Council. He found that, both before and after they were weaned, working-class infants were fed 'sop', bread mashed up with warm water and sugar, and perhaps a little milk. For breakfast and supper, young children of the very poor ate bread which might be covered with treacle or butter, and drank 'so-called' tea. Dinner would be the same or might consist of potatoes, either fried or smeared with a little bacon fat and boiled, or bread spread with dripping (which was the fat melted from roasted meat and which was also sold in shops). The 1904 Report of the Inter-Departmental Committee on Physical Deterioration revealed that, despite the supposed improvements in society and in the condition of the working class that had taken place since Smith's survey, poor children, especially the older ones, still subsisted for the most part on bread eaten with various coverings, such as margarine and jam. Incredibly, in 1936 a rigorously controlled investigation by the Medical Officer of Health for Newcastle into the diets of sixty-nine representative working-class families showed that, after another thirty years of social progress, little had changed. The poor, as they had in the nineteenth-century, still satisfied their hunger with cheap carbohydrate foods, especially bread and margarine washed down with innumerable cups of tea. Another survey carried out in 1936–7 by Sir William Crawford reiterated this finding: bread, the cheapest food, was consumed most

heavily by Class D, the poorest. Twelve per cent of their
expenditure on food was on bread, compared to only three per
cent of that of Class AA, the richest, whilst in relation to
expenditure on meat and fish the reverse was true. The poor also
made heavy use of cheap jams, syrups and sugar, but ate less
fruit. It was disclosures such as these that led John Burnett to
state that, despite the general improvement in standards, the
nutritional inadequacy of the poorest in the Thirties was still
vast and alarming.

One highly crucial discovery of the Newcastle researchers
was that the amount of energy and protein obtained per penny of
money spent on food was twenty-three per cent higher in the
families of the unemployed who were included in the survey
than it was in the families of the employed. This finding went
some way to disproving the assertion that the women of the
urban poor allocated their resources extravagantly. It also
indicated that, within the confines of a choice of food limited not
only by their income but also by the personal tastes of their
husbands and children, many wives tried to make meals as
appetising as possible. It was their aim to put a hot dinner of
some kind or other on the table each day, if it was only Oxo and
potatoes, as one Birmingham woman recalled. Bones were
another favourite resort of her mother's at times of want. These
would be boiled with potatoes to make a stew, the sparse meat on
them having to satisfy a large and hungry family. Women of this
kind succeeded in spite of their poverty, their spirit and
imagination conquering adversity when it would have been so
easy to succumb and to abandon hope and pride. Grace Foakes's
mother was of this mould. She made a bacon pudding out of two
pennyworth of fat bacon pieces, dripping and flour, and in her
rice puddings water had to make do instead of milk. Another
creation of hers was a 'dish' which she called 'pepper and salt
slosh'. This consisted of a slice of bread over which boiling
water was poured, allowed to soak in and the excess drained off.
The addition of a knob of margarine and a sprinkling of salt and
pepper produced a meal very similar to the sop described by Dr
Smith in the 1860s. According to the oral evidence, in Birmingham too such a 'meal' lingered on into the 1930s. It was still
called sop and was made from a slice of bread which was mashed
up with hot water and over which the drippings of the tea pot

were poured. In Salford the equivalent was called 'brewis' and differed only in that the tea was replaced by salted dripping.

Economy dominated the lives of nearly all women who lived in poor neighbourhoods. Stale bread and cakes would be bought cheaply from the baker; a man from Studley Street remembered that, even if the bread was bought freshly-baked, his mother would not cut it until it was stale so as to avoid any waste through crumbs when it was cut. 'Speced' – bruised or damaged – fruit or tomatoes were purchased from the greengrocer or fruiterer and, at the end of the day, the bits of cheese left from its slicing would be sold by the grocer. From the fishmonger, cods' heads might be a cheap purchase with which to make fish cakes; from the tripe shop, 'parings', or bits, and, as we have seen, the butcher sold bones with small amounts of meat on. At his shop could also be bought 'pieces' of meat and, as Catherine Cookson described it, what matter if there was sawdust sticking to the black congealed blood on the meat, or if it was just a piece of the beast's lungs – it made a dinner.

This concept of frugality evaded the notice of Mrs Turpin's health visitor. On one occasion she asked the charlady if she was aware that milk contained all the necessary elements with which to sustain life, and she added that she hoped the children were given a good milk pudding every day. So as to be rid of the unwanted intruder the quicker, the answer was obviously yes. In reality, Mrs Turpin could not provide the milk puddings because she was unable to afford the quart of milk a day which was needed as their main content. Porridge was another meal often recommended by health visitors. Yet to make good and palatable porridge, milk again was needed, as was a sufficient amount of sugar. Furthermore, a decent pot which was not burnt or used for other cooking was essential. In a slum household this was almost impossible. Cooking utensils were usually at a premium, with more than two pots, a frying pan and a kettle unattainable items of expense. Another means of saving money was in the serving of cold meals, because it was too expensive to heat the stove. For the same reason, especially before the First World War, many lower-working-class mothers found it cheaper to pay the local baker twopence to cook the Sunday dinner, rather than to waste fuel on an open fire or gas on the stove in their own house. Despite this inability always to provide the ideal of a hot, cooked meal, it was a fallacy, as shown by the Liverpool survey, that the poor lived out of tins. Apart from condensed milk and cooked meat sold in shops and which had previously been kept in tins, the poor lived on fresh food. Of course, that in itself was more often than not bread, the staple diet of the lower working class, a stale loaf of which when toasted and mashed with tea and plenty of sugar provided an alternative baby food to rusks. Yet nowhere were the economies of the mothers of the urban poor more noticeable than in their attempts to vary this monotonous diet, although still guided by the principle of filling the immediate food wants of the family, rather than necessarily by an attention to the consideration of the nourishment and efficiency provided by the food.

A great number of a wife's purchases were made daily and in tiny quantities – for example, a single egg or an ounce of tea. Indeed, groceries were largely bought by the ounce and meat and fish by the halfpennyworth. Helen Forrester mentioned how she and her brother would tramp for miles to go to a shop which would cut a twopenny, half-pound pack of margarine into quarter-pounds. Obviously, shopkeepers who split up goods could make more money. As Helen Forrester noticed, a sixpenny, one pound pot of jam when sold by the ounce at a penny an ounce assured an excellent profit. In connection with this manner of shopping, John Burnett quoted the case of one family who, in the Edwardian era, were known to have made seventy-two distinct purchases of tea within seven weeks. In fact, the average number of purchases made over the same period by a sample of poor families was twenty-seven. Consequently, in the long term, a lower-working-class wife spent more on her meagre requirements than did housewives belonging to other sections of society.

As we have seen, there were, nevertheless, ways in which food could be bought cheaply, even if in small quantities. In *A London Childhood*, Angela Rodaway brought to mind a 'cut-price' shop in Islington where, by paying careful attention to prices, as much as a shilling could be saved on the week's shopping. There were, particularly, devices which ensured that meat would not be totally absent from the table. A family might keep fowl which, besides providing eggs, could be killed and when boiled made an appetising meal; wild rabbits, skinned on a hawker's cart, could be bought for sixpence around 1914, or they might even be poached, and every lower-working-class neighbourhood seemed to have its 'cheap' butcher.

Robert Sherard mentioned one in connection with the chain-makers of Cradley Heath in his book, *The White Slaves of England*, published in 1897. On the Ladypool Road in Birmingham which was renowned for its butchers, one trader in meat proudly advertised himself outside his shop as 'The Poor Man's Friend'. His type of butcher specialised in selling the cheaper cuts of meat ignored by the 'higher class' butcher who catered for the middle class and, indeed, the more prosperous of the working class. In a place known as the Shambles in Jamaica Row in Birmingham's city centre, a number of these butchers were gathered regularly. Here, before the First World War – and after – a shilling's worth of 'cag-mag' could be bought with which to make a stew for a large family on a Saturday night, the remains of which would be served up for breakfast on Sunday morning. 'Cag-mag' was odds and ends of meat, literally bits and pieces of beef, pork and mutton (the poor could not afford lamb), which were all mixed up together in one parcel and were probably cooked together. Also popular were sheep's heads, with the eyes left in, and pressed cheek, tripe, belly draft, hearts, liver, brains and faggots which could be bought cold before the end of the First World War for three farthings each. Like much of the meat consumed by the poor, faggots consisted of offal, in this case a mixture of liver or pigs' fry with onions, bread and sage. It was also advisable in the case of some of this meat to wipe it with a vinegar cloth and to cook it immediately. The nature of cheap meat meant that cooking time was longer, a fact which made it difficult for many working wives to serve hot meals. A cold meal or bread with a covering of one kind or another was much quicker and simpler for a busy woman to prepare. Nevertheless, many struggled valiantly to provide the ideal, despite their employment, even to the extent of taking a hot basin meal, covered with a red handkerchief, to their husband's works in their own dinner hour. In Salford there was an even cheaper alternative to the cheap butcher; this was the 'slink' butcher. Slink was the flesh of prematurely-born calves, and he (butchers were always men) also sold broxy, the flesh of sheep that had died of disease or accident. The purchase of both of these remained morally repugnant to most of the lower working class, as did that of horse meat, despite their poverty.

There did exist one legitimate way in which mothers of the urban poor could obtain better cuts of meat cheaply, and this was through the habit of late-night shopping. This was common to poor neighbourhoods throughout the country right through the period 1880–1939, and was particularly evident on a Saturday night in Birmingham.

In them days you valued every penny. 'Cus I can remember the days when they give the meat away on a Saturday night. They was open to 10, 11 o'clock at night in them days. No refrigerators in the shops. Whatever meat was left'd be bad before Monday. . . . they couldn't keep it 'cus there were no fridges. They'd be selling it during the course of the day and they'd always got a bloke on the front shouting the odds, the price of meat. And they'd be competing against each other. People round the area would leave it, they wouldn't buy a joint of meat, they'd wait and wait . . . I've seen my mate's mother waiting to be given the meat. They used to start off with half a crown parcels, you know. Come down to two bob. A big joint of beef, p'raps a full string of sausage. Who'd pay half a crown? Almost half a day's wages. They'd wait until the finish until they'd start to cut it up. 'Ee are misses. Wrap that up. Go on, get orf!'. Clear the shop out at the finish. The point is you'd got to bargain . . . [15]

Many churchmen and members of the middle class regarded this habit of late-night shopping as pernicious. They saw it as encouraging women to drink, and by extension as contributing to the neglect of the home, because many wives sat in the pub waiting for the auctioning to begin. In fact, the most these wives could afford to spend on drink was a copper or two on a couple of sticks (a measurement less than a half pint) of beer or a drop of Dunville's whiskey. Without the practice of butchers selling off their remaining stocks of meat cheaply, 'slink' butchers and their like would undoubtedly have become more popular, or else hunger would have become more aggravated and nutrition even worse amongst the poor.

Sound household management was not restricted to contriving to create satisfying meals on severely limited finances. Economies had to be made elsewhere in the family budget, because food consumption could only fall to a certain minimum, no matter how dangerously low for the members of a family that might be. Through a multitude of shifts, a wife of the urban poor exhibited her skills in household management and displayed her success in defying the hostile conditions of slum life. Nappies for a young baby were too dear to buy, so many mothers bought terryline – at sixpence a yard in the 1920s – to make their own, as well as flannelette at threepence a yard with which to make blankets for the infant. Once totally beyond repair, old clothes (which had been bought second-hand anyway) and pieces of rag or linen which could no longer be pawned would be 'bodged' to make rugs. The poor could not afford linoleum to cover the floors of their houses and these pegged rugs, as they were known, were a variegated relief to the cold stone and quarries of most homes. A husband might be encouraged to mend the family's shoes, whilst hard-wearing clogs were popular amongst the urban poor in many parts of England – and not just in the North. If the heel of a man's sock wore out, a woman who could sew repaired it by cutting the shape of the heel out of the top of the sock. A daughter might wish to have her ears pierced, a service that a mother could accomplish with the help of a needle, a piece of cotton, and a cork about a quarter of an inch less than the length of the needle. This latter was threaded with the cotton and gently pushed through the cork. The mother would then hold the bottom of the girl's ear-lobes tightly and push the needle through them up to the cork face, thus completing the operation. No item, then, was wasted under the vigilant eyes of an improvising wife.

Her children were vital allies to a mother in her struggle to manage and to survive. Their wages from full-time work were essential in order to eke out her budget, especially if she was a widow, as was the case with Jack Lannigan's mother. His memories of his childhood in Salford are also included in John Burnett's collection on that subject. Born in 1890, he recollected that after the death of his skilled father the family was thrust into poverty, and he recalled how his mother, though suffering from ill-health, had to take in washing to ensure its survival. At the age of ten Jack successfully sat the school-leaving examination and so started work at six shillings a week, a wage which supplemented his brother's ten shillings a week. The joy with which he greeted his employment speaks volumes about the devotion of children to their mother, and emphasises the argument of this chapter that it was through this devotion that mothers could realise the potential of their power. As Jack Lannigan emotionally put it:

I now wanted to tell the world I was now a man, working and helping my mother . . . After paying the rent, she had no need to go out washing every day, only when she felt like it. How happy she seemed to be. I had not seen her smile for years. If Matt or I received any tips they went to her. She could spend the money better than me, but we received our reward for when we returned home each day there would be some kind of food and soup and now and again a little meat.[16]

Jack Lannigan's sentiments were shared as deeply by Will Crook, as told in George Haw's biography, *From Workhouse to Westminster: The Life Story of Will Crooks MP*. This Labour representative had been born in Poplar in 1852, one of seven children. Whilst he was still young his father lost an arm, so leaving his mother the sole support of her stricken family. Her toils with the needle long into the night so imprinted themselves on Crooks' youthful consciousness that he awaited with fervent impatience the onset of his manhood when he would be able to work for this 'poor sweated woman'.

Yet the financial assistance provided by working children was not dependent on their full-time employment; part-time earnings from jobs carried on whilst they were still at school were another vital source of additional income. As John Gillis understood in *Youth and History*, an adolescent amongst the middle class was a man-child amongst the working class and, as we have seen, women-children were as obvious, if not more so, in that class. An investigation on 'Child employment and juvenile delinquency' by Nettie Adler in 1908 gave resonance to this astute observation. It was included in Gertrude Tuckwell's study, *Women in Industry*, and it revealed that nationally nine per cent of all school children worked outside school hours. This figure did not include half-timers who were very common in Lancashire and who worked for half a day in a mill and went to school for the other half. Neither did it include the children of the very poor who raised money by their own devices rather than through a recognised job. It was the education of these children in particular which was adversely affected by their employment. Often absent from school as a result of their work, and too tired to concentrate on their lessons when they were present, poor children were, as the headmistress of a school in the Studley Street quarter observed in her log book in 1889, 'the failures throughout the school'. The haphazard attendance at school by the children of the urban poor blighted their futures. It drastically hindered their ability to escape their poverty because, badly educated as they were, they became established in the same unskilled, irregular and casual employment that was the bane of their parents' lives. In this way the poor remained prisoners of their poverty.

There were a great number of tasks which could be accomplished by children. In the poor central wards of Birmingham many of these were associated with aspects of industry which lent themselves to the labour of light-fingered, small children. As Robert Sherard noticed in 1905 in *The Child Slaves of England*, for the sheer misery of laborious and underpaid labour in which children were forced to participate as long as their little fingers could move and their eyes could keep open, then the investigator needed to look in the squalid homes of the courts of the city. The kind of industrial outwork at which children were most useful was repetitive, long-drawn-out, and ill-paid: wrapping up hairpins in paper – ten to the paper, with one outside to hold the pack together – at $2\frac{1}{4}d$ a thousand; a penny a day to bend tin clasps around safety pins, which worked out at a halfpenny a gross; carding a gross of safety pins at $2\frac{1}{2}d$ a gross if there were nine pins of different sizes on each card, rising to $4\frac{1}{2}d$ a gross if there were fifteen pins, and five pence a gross if there were eighteen pins, and varnishing pen-holders at $1\frac{1}{2}d$ a gross. Other jobs similar in their fatiguing nature included the carding of hooks and eyes, the papering of pins, and the sewing of buttons onto cards, the wages for all of which, in Sherard's words, could only be calculated by 'infinitesimal fractions of pence'. Long and hard labour was also the unenviable lot of lather boys in barbers' shops who, before 1914, could earn a shilling for twelve hours' work. In the summer holidays other older boys could find employment in beer houses which brewed their own beer. Their job, for up to nine hours a day, was to steam out the casks and scrub out the copper in which the beer was brewed. This was accomplished by climbing into them on ladders and scrubbing them with bucketfuls of silver sand.

This kind of part-time work – if such a phrase can be used in connection with work which was almost full-time in its nature – was obviously not relished, but there were a variety of other means by which ingenious children of school age could earn money for their mothers, or at least rid them for a day of the worry of how to provide their offspring with an evening meal. Selling local newspapers was popular: twelve papers would be bought and the thirteenth given the vendors free. The halfpenny earned from this could buy 'a halfpenny dip' at an eating house: a slice of bread dipped in the tray of fat over which would be roasting a cow's body. Children would also buy mint, rhubarb and the like from those who had gardens and grew them, and would then sell them along shopping thoroughfares for a penny a bunch, and empty wooden boxes would be collected from shops, bundled, and sold as firewood for a halfpenny. No job was too dirty, no task too menial, no opportunity lost in the battle to maximise the housekeeping money. Horse droppings would be collected and sold as fertiliser at a penny a bucket; matches were sold, and the horses of delivery men held – or caught after they had deliberately been made to bolt – for a small reward. A woman from middle-class Moseley in Birmingham even remembered 'ragged urchins' who turned cartwheels in the Bull Ring for a few coppers. Street jobs of this kind were popular because the children themselves determined the nature and extent of their work. They afforded a certain freedom of choice and necessitated an imaginative and resourceful mind, as well as providing the means by which to earn money.

Theft was not always ruled out in the efforts to provide food for a lower-working-class family. Mothers would not be involved in or necessarily instigate this action, but it is obvious that not only hunger but loyalty to an anguished mother desperately trying to provide for her family was an inducement to criminality by a devoted son. A man from a poverty-stricken family in Studley Street, Birmingham, declared that when he was a youth, in the years after 1918, he would 'pinch' anything for his mother. He was a hawker and at night he would take his small barrow round the back of fruit shops and steal boxes of oranges and bananas. One Christmas there was no food in the house so, after drinking in a local pub (like many men food came second to the purchase of beer), he and three friends robbed fowl out of a yard in a more prosperous working-class road. As a youngster, he regularly took eggs from similar fowl pens elsewhere in his area. Most theft was on a much smaller scale, decidedly petty in its nature, and committed by younger children satisfied with a swede, turnip, apple, orange or some other item that was clasped easily by 'sticky fingers' and was as easily hidden from a watchful shopkeeper. The prevalence of open-fronted greengrocers' shops in working-class districts did not make this kind of theft too dangerous.

Stealing of this kind was not regarded as wrong by the poor. Small-scale as it was, and satisfying only immediate hunger, it could be further justified as a child's attempts to help its mother. What is more remarkable is that hordes of slum children did not grow into habitual and inveterate criminals. The temptation must have been great, given the freedom from want that crime for pecuniary gain could provide. An example is provided in the case of a brothel-keeper living in a back-to-back house in a poor part of Birmingham. At the coroner's inquest as to the circumstances of his death on 25 August 1880, it was revealed that, although only out of prison for a month, on the day he died he had eaten a dinner of beef and potatoes, and a supper of beef, bread, cheese, ale and toasted bread – a stark contrast to the normal fare of a labourer living in a lower-working-class neighbourhood. The limiting of crime in these districts, especially large-scale theft and theft of money, was noteworthy and was not a result of the successful implementation of middle-class codes of conduct, neither was it through a fear of the law and the police. Instead, it was a direct consequence of the self-regulation of the poor according to their own concepts of right and wrong, concepts of which matriarchs were the guardians and also often the originators. This is emphasised by the case of Arthur Harding, a violent and dangerous criminal. This man was born in 1886 in 'The Nichol', a notorious and feared quarter of Bethnal Green made infamous by Arthur Morrison's fictionalised account of it in *A Child of the Jago*. Harding grew up to become the 'terror of Brick Lane', yet, despite the opportunity thus given him to steal for personal gain, he stole only enough to provide for his mother and sister. Whether or not Harding really did restrain himself in this way, the acceptance of the notion that he should is illuminating.

Despite all contrivances and economies, and notwithstanding the help of neighbours and the earnings of children, even the most adroit wife could not forever hold at bay the spectre of debt. This haunted many an able woman as much as it did those less dextrous in making ends meet. A wife shrewd in the handling of money, efficient in the cutting down of waste, and clever in the purchase of good food cheaply, still balanced a very fine budget. Any diminution in this could seriously affect her ability to stave off the readily-available option of credit. The illness, injury, unemployment or death of a wage-earner, whether male or female, especially if that person contributed the most money to the housekeeping, was a disaster which ensured that the family would never be free of the credit offered by the corner shop, or the money loaned by the pawnbroker and perhaps the moneylender. Charles Booth noted that nearly all his examples of poorer families admitted spending weekly more than was earned. He gave two explanations for this: firstly, that regular earnings were understated, and, secondly, that credit was necessary, the debts of which could be met either by a final evasion of indebtedness or by some windfall outside the regular earnings. It is little wonder that gambling, especially on horses, appealed to so many of the poor as a means by which a small outlay could achieve that windfall.

One last option offered itself to a wife before she need fall into debt: that of not paying the landlord any rent until the family's financial situation improved, at which time, hopefully, the arrears could be paid off. This was a very tempting solution to adopt because if that monetary betterment did not transpire the family could move home. Before 1914 empty houses were common in poor neighbourhoods so that most moves were within the same quarter, often within the same street, a fact which encouraged the growth of 'settled' communities. Women especially were loath to move away from relatives and neighbours and, if they were respected, to abandon the advantages conferred by being known. Yet even after adopting this strategy, by which no stigma attached itself to the family according to the standards of morality prevailing amongst the poor, many wives could still not manage to feed their families. It was at this stage that a wife's standing in the community and the respect or otherwise accorded to her became so important, for the next tactic available was that of receiving goods on credit from the local corner shop. This, known variously as on the 'tick', 'slate', 'strap' or 'mace', would be granted only if a woman's reputation was sound and the shopkeeper believed that he or she would, at some stage, receive their payment. Knowledge of this kind could only be gained if the applicant was known in the community and it was for this reason that strangers to a district joined those whose prestige was low in their inability to obtain credit.

Corner shops became a vital means of survival to a lower-working-class mother. Robert Roberts explained the predicament of Maggie Carey, one of his mother's 'tick' customers at her corner shop. Mr Carey earned eighteen shillings a week, out of which he retained 2s 6d for beer and tobacco. This left his wife the sum of 15s 6d, with which it was impossible to manage a family of nine, even taking into consideration the two shillings earned by one son at a part-time job in the winter. As Roberts commented, a woman of worth and an intelligent illiterate, Maggie Carey looked on the credit connection with his mother's shop as a life-line. It was a sentiment shared by most other wives of the urban poor. To maintain this life-line and to ensure continued credit, it was necessary that each week the previous week's bill at the shop was paid, in part if not in full. As a result, the first call on the housekeeping, taking precedence over the demands of the landlord, was the settlement of this debt. A woman who consistently paid enhanced her status within her community. Obviously there were dangers inherent in this kind of system. For the imprudent wife, the use of the facilities of credit offered by the corner shop and also the pawnbroker could become an easy option, preventing her from attempting to manage her finances wisely, whilst for other women resort to them continued as a habit even after the earnings provided by working children should have allowed it to lapse. This was the case of one woman in Studley Street, Birmingham:

Well, everybody was poor . . . but yes they were very poor in Studley Street . . . The Ms, they was very poor, they was starving. But the old lady was a very bad manager, very bad manager. I don't know what she used to do with her money . . . her used to have everythink on the knock, the shop in Ombersley Road, Tuckies. Well, Wally had grown up and he found out that his mother kept having stuff on the knock and her'd got a big bill . . . Her'd got no money.

Well, he took his mother with him and went up to Tuckies and he said,
  'Now, I want that bill paid and don't let her have nothing else
without paying for it, 'cus I shan't pay for it again.'
Course they didn't, but she found somewhere else.[17]

Another advantage of the corner shop was that, although
prices might be a little higher than in shops along main
thoroughfares, it was possible to purchase from the proprietor
the tiniest amounts of food, from a single rasher of bacon to a
halfpenny worth of milk. For this reason, and the important one
of the extension of credit, Co-operative stores were not generally used by the poor. They drew their clientèle instead from an
upper working class who could afford to be thrifty and who
were, as a consequence, attracted by the dividend. Finally, and
importantly for the cohesion of a street or quarter, the corner
shop offered itself as an important social centre for the
community. Here, as well as on the street and in the beer house,
women – particularly matriarchs – could meet and discuss local
events.

All corner shops were of the 'huckster' type. That is, they sold
nearly everything apart from meat (except in the form of bacon).
One item they did not provide was ready cash, and this omission
was happily filled by the pawnbrokers. Like owners of corner
shops, they did not cater solely for the poor. Any person in
difficult circumstances and who had goods which could be
pledged was welcome, yet it was the urban poor who were the
regular and consistent customers of the pawnbroker. As
Melanie Tebbut has explained, pawnbroking was an essentially
urban phenomenon. In 1870 the greatest density of pawnbroking
licences per county was in Lancashire, which provided twenty-
seven per cent of the total number of licences. Most of these
were to be found in the heavily industrialised south of the
county: 248 in Manchester, the highest concentration outside
London, and 189 in Liverpool, the third largest total for a city.
With a total of 240 pawnshops, the equally industrial Warwickshire boasted the highest proportion of pledge shops per head
of population, a ratio of one pawnshop per 2,656 people. Indeed,
218 of the county's premises were to be found in Birmingham,
the industrial capital of the Midlands. Other manufacturing
areas were also remarkable for the number of pawnbrokers: the
Black Country; the Potteries; Yorkshire, mostly in the coastal

towns and in Leeds, Bradford and Sheffield, and Durham and Northumberland.

The trade itself divided into a more respectable 'city' section and a less respectable 'district' section, the shops of which were to be found in poorer neighbourhoods and catered for the lower working class. These latter were very much part of the local community, much more so than were banks, and their owners were normally on sociable terms with their customers. Along with the trade in general, they went into almost terminal decline after the First World War, but they remained a familiar sight in poorer quarters right through the 1920s and 1930s. They also remained a crucial support for many wives distracted by the inadequacies of their housekeeping money. However, once unfavourable circumstances had forced a woman into pawning a possession, then the routine of redeeming it on a Saturday on receipt of her own or her husband's wages, only to pledge it again on the following Monday, became a difficult one to break:

The pawnbroker? There used to be one on Stoney Lane ... Etty Bennett's. There used to be a queue outside there Monday morning. All round Studley Street and there, mother, Mrs Bird and one or two of the others, they'd go and get a basket carriage from Toomb's and go round the houses in Studley Street and collect the bundles orf the women. And they'd wheel it down the pawn shop ... and get in the queue and get as much as they could ... Used to get it out of a Saturday and tek it back again Monday.[18]

Pawnshops in poorer localities rarely closed before twelve o'clock on a Saturday night, but as the payment of wages on a Friday became more widespread during the inter-war years, then it came to be replaced by Friday as the heaviest redemption day. Monday still remained, however, the busiest day for pledges, and Melanie Tebbut quoted the case of one small local shop which registered three times as many pledges on that day as on any other.

Throughout the period 1880–1939, washing and items of clothing provided the bulk of pledges in poor neighbourhoods, but they were not the only possessions which were pawned. Any item on which a pawnbroker would advance a loan was a financial asset which at some time or other a wife might need to capitalise on. A particularly poignant belonging which was pledged regularly by many women was their wedding ring. The pawning of this was probably one of the worst experiences a wife could suffer; a Birmingham woman remembered tearfully how her mother had died without a wedding ring on her finger, it having been pawned so many times that eventually it remained unredeemed and so became the property of the pawnbroker. Angela Rodaway recalled that it was believed locally that whilst one woman's wedding ring was in pawn she slept in the front room on the sofa; once she had it back she could then sleep with her husband like a normal wife. Yet, when desperate, a mother's primary concern was with the welfare of her children, and before this priority her own pride had to take second place. In Birmingham, brass imitation rings could be bought for a few coppers and this device was obviously extensively resorted to throughout urban England. Walter Greenwood mentioned it in relation to Manchester, and Melanie Tebbut reported that, in 1875 in Liverpool, ninety per cent of the customers of one pawnbroker wore brass wedding rings. This observation also emphasises the fact that most customers of pawnbrokers were women. Faced with husbands who did not understand their difficulties in managing on their income, many wives had to pawn goods discreetly without their husbands' knowledge. This meant that a woman's worries were exacerbated, especially if she could not afford to redeem her partner's suit in time for him to wear it on Sunday. Her failure to do so could lead to her suffering both emotionally and physically.

Another unhappy realisation for a hard-pressed wife was that pawning was most expensive for those caught in the weekly cycle of pledging to redeem. An Act of Parliament of 1872 laid down that the interest charged by a pawnbroker was to be twenty-five per cent per annum for loans under two pounds, or a halfpenny a month for each two shillings lent or fractions of that sum. This latter provision meant that the annual rate of interest could be massively higher than that laid down by the Act. Melanie Tebbut graphically illustrated how it was that the smaller the loan, the higher was the interest, and at the same time she showed that the heavier rate fell most on those who could least afford to pay it. She quoted the instance of a bundle on which ten shillings was lent. The charges on this were $2\frac{1}{2}d$ interest a month, and a halfpenny for the pawn ticket. After a month of weekly pledging, the woman who pawned this bundle would be eleven shillings down; after two months she would be twelve shillings down, and after three months thirteen shillings down. The inevitable result was that the deficit had to be made up with the pawning of another bundle.

Pawning did provide some women in poor neighbourhoods with the means of making money, not losing it. Arthur Harding recalled that in the East End of London, women who collected bundles for pledging were paid for their trouble, and Walter Greenwood mentioned this happening in the North-West. He also indicated the reason for this apparently wasteful expend-iture, for with pawnshops so common in lower-working-class quarters it would seem a foolish and extravagant gesture to pay another for a task which a woman or her children could easily carry out themselves. In Greenwood's novel, Mrs Nattle is the local woman who pawns on commission for neighbours, and her clients are 'too high and mighty' to go to the pawnshop themselves. Shy and retiring women for the most part, their consciences never would have forgiven them for entering a pawnshop. My oral evidence from Birmingham also indicates that certain women pawned on commission for those who would have been socially embarrassed to pledge their own bundles. These were wives who would have regarded the open act of their pawning as a public acknowledgement of their straitened circumstances and redolent with implications as to their loss of status. The earlier quote referring to Studley Street also indicates another aspect which is relevant to this question of pawning for others. The women mentioned in this oral testi-mony were matriarchs and carried out their duty free. It could be argued that their action and the assistance offered by it to mothers with young children, the ill and the infirm was another example of their responsibility to their community.

There was available to wives another way of raising money with which she could feed her family. This was provided by the local money-lender. There were two kinds of money-lender: those who were legally registered and those who were not. Melanie Tebbut, in a very perceptive analogy, has described the ethical position of street money-lenders as comparable to that of back-street abortionists; both services arose out of the desperation of the working class, both aroused the ire of philanthropists, but both received the uncertain gratitude of the community. Another similarity was that practitioners of both were usually women. Booth mentioned one deprived area in his study in which every street had a money-lender, often a woman, and my oral evidence suggests that his observation was as true for the slum neighbourhoods of Birmingham in the 1930s as it had been for London in the 1880s, although it is difficult to distinguish whether or not a money-lender was registered or not. Studley Street certainly had its own female money-lender, at least up until the 1940s, and Jerry White reported that in Campbell Bunk in the 1920s and 1930s there were at least six recognised money-lenders, all of them women. Walter Greenwood's Mrs Nattle was also described as a woman who 'obliged' neighbours, and it would appear that money-lenders were familiar figures in poorer areas throughout England's towns and cities.

Many money-lenders were lower working class themselves and were distinguished from their neighbours by circumstances which made them financially slightly more fortunate. They were often spinsters who, if they worked, had considerably less expense than did the wife and mother of a large family. As Melanie Tebbut has shown, they could also have been women whose husbands were paid on a Friday and so could afford to lend a small sum to their neighbours whose husbands were paid on a Saturday, or else they might have been women who were widowed in the First World War and who were in receipt of a government pension. Once established as a money-lender, then the operation of their business became self-financing, for in settled, tightly-knit communities the urban poor placed the highest importance on honouring small debts, particularly those between themselves. During the 1920s a man from Studley Street remembered that his mother borrowed 2s 6d each week, year after year, from the street's money-lender. The interest charged on this kind of loan was exorbitant, at least a penny in the shilling, which worked out at an annual rate of interest of 433·5%. Yet this woman would no more have thought of reneging on her debt than she would have done of leaving the street. To have done either would have meant the loss of her position within the community.

Arthur Harding's sister, Mighty, was a successful example of the unmarried woman of the urban poor who resorted to money-lending to alleviate her family's poverty. Her prowess at earning money was marked: she also rented out lace curtains, and to other women she sold Provident cheques worth twenty-one shillings at the rate of a shilling a week for twenty-two weeks, thus realising a profit of a shilling on each. Additionally, she received a commission of 1s 8d on each cheque she sold from the large store at which they had to be spent. This easy-payment scheme had been introduced in 1881 by the Provident Clothing Company and, to the women who availed themselves of its facilities, it gave a spending power they had never previously enjoyed, for on payment of the first shilling the cheque and all it offered was handed over to them.

When discussing means of credit, it is important to be aware that, in spite of their impoverishment, wives of the urban poor could and did attempt to insure themselves against hard times through saving. This form of protection was not with a friendly society or an insurance company; rather it was achieved through small, highly localised groups of lower-working-class women. A group of wives would bond together and form a club, known as a 'didly club' in Lambeth and a 'didlum' club in Birmingham. Out of their number, one who was trusted by all would be chosen to hold the cash and to distribute it at the appointed time, usually Christmas. Properly known as 'rotating credit associations', the payments increased by the sum paid in the first week. Thus if a figure of a halfpenny was decided on – usually the case by the 1920s – then in the first week a halfpenny was saved, in the next a penny, and so on. If a member paid up for the full fifty weeks in which the club ran, then a sum of £2 13s 1½d was saved. For most women it was a struggle to keep up these payments throughout the full term, but even those who dropped out before the allotted term still received a not insignificant sum to help them out.

The colloquial names of these clubs are probably derived from the belief that those entrusted with clubs' funds 'diddled' or cheated their members out of their money. This belief arose because of the disappearance of some trustees with the collection and also because some clubs were in the habit of paying the collectors with the final week's fee. Yet such clubs were – and still are – very popular and if swindles had been common place then they would soon have ceased to exist. The fact that they persisted, then, is another indication not only of the self-help evident amongst lower-working-class wives but also of the role of matriarchs within their communities. Trust and respect were essential qualities required in those entrusted with the funds, and these were both attributes much in evidence in matriarchs who were, anyway, normally distinguished by their length of residence in a neighbourhood.

The Harding family were also expert at supplementing their income with the assistance granted them by charities. Arthur's father was adept at 'cadging', that is duping these organisations, whilst he described his mother as a forager. She was aware that if the family was to fool these charities into helping out, not just during occasional times of want but continually, then it was necessary to make her family's poverty known to those who doled out relief. A prerequisite of this was that both parents and children needed to appear as deserving of help; they had to be seen as poor as a result of misfortune and not as a result of their own personal failings. A plethora of charities which could be used by families such as the Hardings existed in every centre of population. As Dr Robertson remarked of the Floodgate Street area of Birmingham in 1904, anyone who inspected it could not fail to be impressed at the number of agencies – religious and social – which were aiming at the betterment of the people. As in the case of the Birmingham Women's Settlement, founded in 1899 and based in Summer Lane, this was directed at improving the moral and intellectual welfare of the poor as much as in providing for their physical well-being.

Most lower-working-class families were not as systematic as the Hardings in their approach to charities, indeed these latter banded together in a Charities Organising Committee to prevent their kind of misuse of their help. Nevertheless, it was a rare mother of the poor who did not, at some time, have recourse to seeking the aid of one or other of the many types of agencies, especially for help for her children. In Birmingham the young of the lower working class were, in most cases, easily distinguishable by their dress. A local paper, the Daily Mail, provided shoes for girls and boots for boys. This footwear had pinholes in it which formed a number and which also served to identify it to pawnbrokers. City bye-laws prevented them from accepting these boots and shoes as pledges. The Police-Aided Association for Clothing Children supplied kilts for girls, corduroy trousers for boys, and jerseys for both. How deep a family's poverty was could be determined by the extent to which a child was clothed by these two charities. The footwear was widely distributed and it was largely because of this that barefooted children disappeared from the streets of Birmingham. Consequently, little stigma was attached to its wearing as most poor children were at some time in receipt of the Daily Mail's benevolence. In winter, churches, schools and sometimes groups of influential shop-keepers would provide soup for the young of the lower working class who were deemed needy. During term-time they might also be the beneficiaries of free breakfasts, consisting of a mug of cocoa and a thick slice of bread and jam, served at a school centrally placed in each district. At Christmas one charity dished up thousands of free hot dinners, including meat as well as vegetables, at Bingley Hall in the city centre for these same children. In another section of the Hall toys were given away. A ticket was the means whereby all the instances of charity quoted were secured by a child. These tickets would be handed out by teachers and health visitors, and in the case of those agencies based in a certain neighbourhood, by a clergyman, doctor, wealthy and successful shopkeeper or some other worthy of the middle class important in the district.

No organisation existed which could compare with the welfare state of today, although from 1911 governments began to take the first tentative steps towards a national system of relief based on funding from the central government. Thus during the 1920s and 1930s state benefits, associated with the notorious Means Test in the latter decade, existed side-by-side with the established local system of parish relief. This latter provided indoor relief for the destitute poor in the workhouse, and also outdoor relief in their own homes to those of the poor who were regarded as requiring temporary help. It was this form of state-inspired, though locally-funded, relief that was more familiar to the lower working class. In contrast to the parish, the Means Test became familiar to all of the working class, doling out money – forty-three shillings in the case of the Forrester family of nine in the 1930s – once an unemployed man had exhausted his savings and sold all non-essential items of furniture. The parish gave only vouchers – the poor could not be trusted to spend money wisely – and these could be redeemed for food or coal. A sense of humiliation existed in applying to the parish. This was induced firstly by an adult's feeling of failure (that is if they did not subscribe to the Harding parents' philosophy). Secondly, the attitude of some members of the panel who decided whether or not a family should receive benefit was often hostile towards an applicant. In *96 Years a Brummie* by Tom Golding, his mother, who was born in 1890, remembered how it was necessary to plead for assistance from the panel, the members of which would ask searching questions of the person making the request for help. Thirdly, the parish and the Means Test made use of the services of 'visitors', whom the poor regarded as outsiders who were sent to spy on them. Visitors had become increasingly familiar to the poor during the Edwardian age. At the birth of each baby in a lower-working-class family, a health visitor – later the welfare – would call. In the case of large families, visits were not dependent on a birth, they were regular. This entry into a home, which a man could not prevent, and the tacit or spoken judgements made on a family's life-style incensed many husbands as an infringement of their authority and an insult to their wives' cleanliness. A Birmingham woman recalled how her father vehemently objected to the calls of a visitor, although she occasionally brought with her toys for the children who would otherwise have had none. His wife kept the home spotless, he was hard-working and he regarded it as an affront to his dignity that anyone should be able to enter his house and 'snoop' around without his permission.

Visitors employed by the parish and the Means Test were as deeply resented. Many of the lower working class supplemented this form of assistance with part-time jobs, the earnings of which they illegally did not declare, as was the case with Kathleen Dayuss's father. Visits were often unannounced in the hope of catching the offenders out, but the poor in their close communities had their own means of countering this tactic. A woman from Ladywood in Birmingham was left a widow with three young children in the late 1930s. She brought to mind how her neighbours helped her as she sought to add to her widow's pension of a pound, plus twenty-one shillings relief:

I was forever having washing . . . and do all the grates, scrub the floors. I used to get more money that way. It was only like a big yard, Stoke Street was and they used to say,
  'Liz, somebody's about, stranger's knocking about!'
I used to run upstairs and shift all the washing. Anyway,
  'Oh, there's a stranger around!' Mrs Cottam said,
  'Well', I said, 'I'm alright, I've got nothing hanging about.'
So her (the visitor) comes in. I go's upstairs and her follows me up and she says
  'Haven't you got a tablecloth?'
I said,
  'Yes, I've got a tablecloth . . . makes the room look a bit better.'
  'Oh', she said, 'You've got extra food here, I see.'
'Cus Mrs Cottam used to bring me up a saucepan of her stew; I said,
  'I've had it give me.'
  'Oh', she says, sommut else that upset me.
I said,
  'Look! There's the door!' I said 'Piss orf!'
  I said, 'And don't come here no more!'
  I said, 'My kids've never wanted for nothing, not while I've got these!' (her hands)
  And she said, 'Don't you take that attitude with me . . . You'll be in front of the committee.' . . . So anyway, they had me in front of the committee 'cus I had to hand me book in. He said, 'You can't do this, take this attitude, bouncing with visitors.'
I said, 'I can do what I like!'[19]

This episode forcefully emphasises much of the argument of this chapter: the devotion of mothers to their children; their hard work and self-sacrifice; their self-help and that of the community, and their attempts to remain independent and proud. Finally, this woman's reaction was to return to work in a factory and it was through the earning of their own money that many lower-working-class mothers increased their independence and expanded their potential to exert power and influence.

Chapter three

Independent women

Despite the massive restraints on freedom imposed by the shackles of poverty, to many who worked amongst the lower working class the women of the urban poor appeared as frighteningly independent. As with much else pertaining to the way of life of this section of society, this independence had always been present, but was now more obvious in the wake of numerous surveys and studies. In 1901 a Superintendent of a Church Mission amongst the poor, who were as much the subject of missionary activity as were African and Asian nations, summed up the opinion of those of the middle class who regarded the apparent freedom of action enjoyed by lower-working-class women as posing a danger to the established order of English society. Mr Wheatley believed that the position of all women amongst the urban poor:

... has undergone, and is now undergoing, a great change ... Women are entering into competition with men more and more and their old subordination to and dependence on men is fast disappearing ... they act in almost every respect with the same freedom as men ... And when these women marry or go to live with a man they do not stay at home and look after the house or children. They turn out to go to work in factory or laundry; the home is neglected and the children, if there are any, are put out to be looked after, or to roam the streets if they are old enough. The modern woman of the poorer classes cannot stay at home, it is too dull, the surroundings too depressing, she likes to get into the lively circle of the factory room.[20]

Compared with upper-working-class and middle-class women, those of the urban poor were more self-reliant and less dependent on men, whether husbands or fathers. Indeed, although social progress is usually seen as a process which begins at the most prosperous and educated reaches of society, eventually percolating to the poor and least educated, in respect of the freedom and power wielded by women the reverse was true. It can be argued that in this field the affluent followed in the furrow ploughed by the lower working class. Whilst some middle-class women were striving to secure the franchise for their sex in the belief that this was a kind of Holy Grail, the attainment of which would precipitate their social as well as political emancipation, the women of the urban poor were, in many respects, already in control of their own destinies. This control was achieved through the securing of their own income through paid employment.

The 1901 census numbered over four million women who were at work in England and Wales. All but 300,000 or so of these were engaged in 'working-class' jobs, that is they were employed in domestic service or in industry. Middle-class moralists had little to complain of with regard to the former employment, believing that domestic service induced respect for their 'betters' amongst the poor. It was notable in the industrial towns and cities, however, that this kind of occupation did not appeal to the young women of the lower working class, who instead preferred to find work in factories. The fear of these moralists was that social control would be more difficult to exert in what was regarded as the 'freer' atmosphere of the factory shop, whilst the imposition of middle-class standards of behaviour would be rendered correspondingly harder. Yet this new phenomenon, as it was perceived at the close of the century, was not in fact novel. The Industrial Revolution had opened up alternative employment to agricultural work and domestic service as much to working-class women as it had to men. Friedrich Engels had observed this in the textile industry in Lancashire during the 1840s, and in 1857, at a conference organised by the National Association for the Promotion of Social Science, it was stated that the industrial employment of women was by then a reality. To add support to this assertion, it was revealed that in Great Britain as a whole three-quarters of the adult unmarried women, two-thirds of widows and one-seventh of married women were earning their bread by independent labour. Their number could be supplemented if all those women who shared in the 'ordinary industrial avocations' of their families were included.

A feature of industrial employment for women, from its earliest beginnings and throughout the period 1880–1939, was that it was restricted to the working class. Furthermore, in general only the 'meanest' occupations – the least skilled, most arduous and often dirtiest of jobs – were made available to women. The higher stations of industry where skill was dominant were usually to remain the preserve of men. Promotion to these better-paid jobs became effectively disbarred to women who, like youngsters to whose wages their own tended to gravitate, were regarded as a pool of cheap labour. During 1888 Dr Hill, Birmingham's first Medical Officer of Health, commissioned a report on 'sweating' – the employment of labour for long hours under poor conditions and at starvation wages. In the six 'sweat shops' where the sexes were distinguished separately, thirty-seven women were employed, compared with fifteen men and two boys. A later report in 1906 concentrated on an inspection of workshops. These were smaller than factories and provided much employment for women in conditions that were described as unwholesome. In nearly all cases, the workshops were old, badly arranged, dark and ill-ventilated.

Working women were especially essential to the industry of Birmingham. As early as 1857 it was believed that the suspension of female labour, described as an 'institution' of the city, would lead to an 'annihilation' of many of the trades for which it was famous. Sixty-five years later, the very general employment of women remained not only one of Birmingham's social peculiarities but was regarded as abnormally high. It had been revealed in 1893 that the number of girls aged between ten and fifteen who were employed in the city was nineteen per cent higher than the national average. More significantly, the number of girls aged between fifteen and twenty who were working was a staggering eighty per cent higher than the national average. Seminally, the importance of the female workforce did not enhance the status of working women, nor did it lead to a rise in their wages. A study in 1906 by E. Cadbury, M. Cecile Matheson and G. Shann, entitled *Women's Work and Wages: A Phase of Life in an Industrial City*, emphasised this. It was disclosed that in 1901 the average wage for a girl of seventeen who was working in Birmingham was ten shillings a week. The authors regarded this as four shillings a week less than the amount which was regarded as necessary if a girl was to keep herself healthy and respectable. For adult women the position was as bad; the average weekly earnings in 1905 for a woman over twenty-one employed in the city's cycle industry was 10s 6d, with 11s 6d constituting the average income for those women working in the bedstead industry.

The wages of most of the female workforce in England's cities and towns were kept low by a number of factors. Firstly, male trade-unions, intent on protecting their normally skilled members, conspired with employers, who were already loath to train women as they feared a loss of their labour through pregnancy or the demands of young children, to prevent their learning a skill. One of the unions most vehement in its opposition to the employment of women in industry was the Birmingham-based National Union of Brass Workers and Metal Mechanics. Its steadfast determination to disbar women from work in the metal trades was recorded in Barbara Drake's extensive study, *Women in Trade Unions*, first published in 1920. The union justified its stance on the grounds that such employment was unhealthy and unsuitable for women, and that the introduction of female labour into a trade resulted in the fall of men's wages and often their unemployment. This attitude so successfully affected the policy of the Amalgamated Society of Engineers that it was not until 1943 that its successor, the Amalgamated Engineering Union, allowed women to become members. Custom, a belief that different standards of life applied to men and women, self-interest, and an adherence to the notion of female inferiority in physical strength and mental ingenuity, all combined then to confirm the acceptance of the notion that women were suited only to unskilled work.

A second factor influential in the maintenance of low wages for female labour was the attitude of some of the women who worked in poorly-paid jobs. There had always been those, like the working girls described in Ship Street, who were uninterested in their work and who changed their employment frequently. A consequence of this was not only that the most unskilled and least well-paid occupations were the only ones available to unstable labour, but that the prejudices of male workers against their female counterparts were vindicated – at least in their own minds. A third cause of poor wages was the

poverty of many working women. In *The Nether World*, one of
Gissing's characters explained that the girls of the lower orders
had to go out to work to earn their own livings, that only the
daughters of the rich could be indulged as children until they
married. The earnings of working girls and women were vitally
important to the literal survival of many poor families and thus
any job, no matter how low the wages, was preferable to none, so
long as it increased the family's income. This fact was con-
tributory in rendering more difficult the organisation of female
labour into trade-unions which might have ameliorated their
working conditions and bettered their pay. Women who
accepted low-paid employment could not afford the luxury of
dissenting from the opinions of their employers, and if that was
against unions there could be little protest, because plenty of
women were desperate enough for work, no matter how low the
rates of pay, to provide replacements for recalcitrant
employees. This problem facing trade-union organisers was
exacerbated by the dispersal of many women workers in small
workshops – precisely those that were most likely to pay least
well. The scattered nature of female employees was noticeable
in many industrial centres, but was particularly evident in
Birmingham. The figures for the 1901 census showed that if
Aston Manor, Smethwick, Handsworth and Kings Norton were
included, then nearly 118,000 women worked in the city. This
was almost forty per cent of the total number of women in the
whole area. Of those in work, fifty-three per cent were employed
in different manufacturing processes, yet only eight per cent of
the total female workforce was estimated by Cadbury and his co-
authors to be members of various preventative clubs. The
example of the pen-making industry illustrated the weakness of
trade-unions in the city. A union for women pen-workers was
formed in 1895 which, having fallen into abeyance, was re-
started in 1898 with dues of twopence a week. A year later
membership peaked at nine hundred, falling rapidly to an
ineffectual five by 1906.

Elsewhere in the country some success was achieved by
women's trade-unions, although this was noticeable under
industrial conditions different from those prevailing in
Birmingham. In Booth's study, Clara E. Collet contributed an
article entitled 'The trades of East London connected with

poverty', wherein she described the achievements of girls making matches for Bryant and May. A prolonged strike in July 1888 had led to the formation of the largest existing union in England and Wales which was composed entirely of women and girls. There were 800 members of the union, of whom 650 paid their dues regularly. The strength of this union was the result of two factors: firstly, the fact that most of the members worked for one employer and, secondly, the unity of the workforce. Many of them lived closely together in the East End, a fact which facilitated the creation of an *esprit de corps*, so vital if a woman worker was to place loyalty to her workmates before loyalty to her family. The match girls had always shown a remarkable power of combination: one girl's grievance became that of all the girls employed in the same factory room, who would often also all be members of a savings club through which clothes and hat feathers were bought. It was this sense of belonging to each other which facilitated the creation and relative durability of their union, although in 1903 – like many other women's unions – it disappeared.

In 1874, through the initiative of Emma Patterson, a Women's Trade Union League had been founded. Its aim was to help in the setting-up of women's trade-unions but, once established, to allow them to be independent and self-supporting. Although for many years it was dominated in its leadership by middle-class enthusiasts, at the grassroots level, away from the public speeches, newspaper reports and articles, working-class women worked vigorously to make it a success. By 1906 the League could count 167,000 members, but the majority of these were better-paid women workers in Lancashire's cotton mills. Indeed, ten years earlier the Report on Trade Unions graphically showed the importance of this group of workers to women's trade-unionism, when it revealed that the 90,000 or so women members of the cotton unions represented five-sixths of all organised women workers. In the very informative *One Hand Tied Behind Us. The Rise of the Women's Suffrage Movement*, Jill Liddington and Jill Norris emphasised the singularity of these women. From 1884, when the Weavers' Amalgamation was formed, until 1914 and the beginning of the decline of the cotton industry, their position was far stronger than that of any other group of working women, their wages were far higher and they were far more likely to be organised into a local association. By 1900 no fewer than a quarter of a million women were employed in the cotton mills and, against the current trend, many of them were employed in skilled and well-paid work. It must be noted, however, that even in Lancashire, by forbidding the employment of women in the spinning room, men retained a monopoly on the highest-paid work.

Female cotton-workers were not the only skilled women workers in England. In London, Arthur Harding recalled that a woman french polisher could earn more money than a male cabinet-maker. Though the work was irregular and hard, it was skilled and paid well and it attracted scores of young women who seemed to possess the almost uncanny touch necessary for the trade. In fact, Harding believed that many young men – he called them 'hooligans' – married french polishers precisely because their wives could earn good money staining the cabinets that they had made. There were also women french polishers in Birmingham, around 400 by 1914, although the brass workers' union was assiduous in its efforts to halt their employment. Even in a city in which skilled and well-paid work for women was at a premium, there were other occupations open to women which enabled them to earn good money: paper-box making, leather-work, brush-making, burnishing, and lathe-work which, though dirty, dangerous and unhealthy, was skilled work. Better-paid occupations for women were not, then, restricted to Lancashire's cotton industry, nor did the general trend in favour of female labour in that county preclude unskilled and underpaid work for women. As Liddington and Norris wrote with qualification, whilst women cotton-workers enjoyed an independence which women elsewhere could not match, it was limited, varying from town to town and according to the marital status of the woman concerned.

In particular this limitation was affected by the position of women employees within the rigid hierarchical structure which impressed itself on all jobs in the mill. According to Robert Roberts, female weavers came 'top of the class', and this is confirmed by Liddington and Norris. At the turn of the century they could earn around twenty-one shillings a week, still less than male weavers, but considerably more than the averages paid to women in the Birmingham industries quoted by Cadbury and his associates. Following female weavers came winders, who could earn about nineteen shillings a week, and drawers-in. Next came card-room workers, described by Liddington and Norris as among the toughest women workers in the mill and, finally, at the base of the hierarchy came ring-spinners. These lacked status on several counts. Firstly, in a county in which religion and nationality were potent forces, this job included a strong Irish Catholic element, and these were regarded as inferior to English Protestants within a caste-ridden Edwardian working class. Secondly, the wages – at about fifteen shillings a week – were low, at least for the Lancashire cotton industry. Thirdly, the respectable regarded card-room women as morally careless because, in the heat of their factory shops, they worked barefoot and were dressed in little more than calico shifts. Another fact which influenced their low status was that they came home covered in dust and fluff. In this respect they could be compared with the women stock-barrel smoothers who were employed in Birmingham's gun trade. A writer of an article in *The Birmingham Daily Post* in 1871 declared that this employment was a most unfeminine occupation, scarcely more suitable work for women than was labour in the brickfields or on the pit bank. The job required a worker to cleanse the stock by scraping it all over with pieces of broken glass, and it was reported that the women who worked at this task could be seen on any fine dinner hour in the city's gun quarter. They were easily distinguished, standing in groups, by the fact that their muscular arms were akimbo and their bodies were covered with the fluff of fine shavings.

Robert Roberts intimated that female occupations were linked to social status within the working class, and this opinion was also expressed by Cadbury and his collaborators. They concluded that the employment of women was determined by the 'class' of a girl and that this was fixed before she started work. Their findings were verified in 1914 by a report, *Birmingham Trades for Women and Girls*, which was issued by the Central Care Committee of the city's Education Department. This found that, whilst factory work could not be avoided for working-class girls, the choice of a youngster's occupation depended largely on the district and home from which the girl came. 'Clean', 'light' work was regarded as respectable and socially dignified, and because it was popular the wages for it tended to become depressed. This was aggravated by the fact that its respectable nature encouraged upper-working-class girls to seek it, and these could work for 'pocket money' wages as their earnings were not needed by their families. Warehouse work – wrapping up, sorting, boxing, weighing and packing – was constantly sought after by these girls as it was not only light and clean, but it also provided a link between manual work and the lower-middle-class-dominated clerical occupations. The dirtier a job and the more 'heavy' – that is, physically demanding – it was, the more it repelled the daughters of the better-off of the working class. An arduous task necessitated a masculine strength in women and this resulted in the relegation in importance of a woman's femininity. Consequently, it was this kind of employment which offered itself most to the poor.

The poorer the family of a girl, then the more likely it was that she would be forced into the dirtiest, heaviest, least skilled and worst-paid work. In Salford, the nadir of employment was to be found in the dye-works and in the local flax mill. Working conditions at the latter were notorious and, even in the hard times evident at the turn of the century, it was believed that a woman had to be hard put to take a job in flax where only starvation wages were paid. For a 55½-hour week of arduous toil, a woman was paid nine shillings, with a bonus if she achieved the difficult objective of losing no time, although a successful strike in 1911 resulted in an increase in wages of two shillings a week. A girl helper of eighteen years of age, however, could only expect to receive the meagre sum of five shillings a week. It would appear, then, that in Lancashire, as in Birmingham, the daughters of the poor worked at the least popular, dirtiest and worst-paid jobs, and that this was as evident in the cotton mills – despite their higher wages – as it was elsewhere. It is also interesting to note that Liddington and Norris showed that the working-class suffragists of Lancashire were drawn almost exclusively from the ranks of the weavers and winders, that is, from the best-paid women workers in the cotton mills. In contrast, only two women card-room workers and no ring-spinners are known to have been involved in the women's suffrage movement in the county. Moreover, whilst the local branches of the former provided a ready base for visiting suffrage speakers, the latter are believed to be the only group which never invited a suffrage speaker to come and address them. This lack of involvement, or even interest, in political affairs would accord with the low status of spinners. Their lives, like those of lower-working-class women workers throughout England, were dominated by the need to support their families and, as I have argued earlier, this left no time for involvement in socio-political activity.

The distinction between women workers was dependent, then, on status within the working class, and in particular it was observed by Booth in his survey in relation to single working girls of the urban poor. These he regarded as deviating in a socially dangerous way from those codes of behaviour demanded of women by middle-class and upper-working-class men. They were neither demure and dependent, nor were they deferential and modest. Booth represented them as rough, boisterous, outspoken, warm-hearted and honest, although low in moral standards. Factory girls were noted for a vehement dislike of monotony, for a predilection for drink and for their use of bad language. Egalitarian in spirit, they cared nothing for appearance, wishing only to mix with their equals. Yet Booth made an important social distinction between 'factory girls' and 'girls who worked in factories'. His differentiation approximated to the grading of jobs influenced by a girl's caste, discussed earlier. Factory girls were the daughters of frequently drunken fathers who were irregularly and casually employed; in the case of London, often on the docks. They provided the workforce for the lower grades of labour in a factory and earned between seven and eight shillings a week. Irregular in their attendance, it was believed that they sought to work only with the aim of providing sufficient funds with which to pay for their pleasure: visits to the music hall or 'penny gaffes' ('low' theatres and music halls) and trips to the public houses with their 'young men'. These girls were readily recognised by the freedom of their walk, the numbers of their friends and the shrillness of their laughter. Adorned and decked out in a finery which, though constrained by poverty, was seen as ostentatious, they paraded the streets of poor neighbourhoods apparently untrammelled by conventional notions of decorum. In all aspects they presented a distinct contrast to the quiet, hard-working and 'respectable' girls who worked in factories. These latter belonged to those families who either straddled or lived above the poverty line; their fathers were in regular employment and they themselves earned around eleven shillings a week.

Booth was not alone in recognising 'the factory girl'. In *North and South*, her industrial novel of the 1850s, Mrs Gaskell described the girls who left one Manchester mill as having bold and fearless faces; they laughed loudly and jested, particularly at those who were above them in rank and station. Cadbury and his fellows perceived similar traits in the mass of unskilled girl workers in Birmingham. It was believed that they lived only for the morrow, and that out of their average ten shillings a week wages they spent seven on their keep and the remaining three on their clothes and amusements. Their type persisted into the 1930s and beyond; Helen Forrester wrote of them giggling and gawking and dressed in their cheap finery in Liverpool, and Angela Rodaway also represented them in Islington. She described herself as frightened of these young girls of fourteen and fifteen who laughed loudly and who shouted and pushed each other off the kerb. Indeed, the social standing of her own family within the working class was vividly shown when her mother threatened that she too would become a factory girl if she did not pass her scholarship examination. In fact, it was little wonder that lower-working-class girls were flighty, care-less, noisy and pleasure-seeking. The reason why they acted like this was correctly interpreted by Richard Hoggart in *The Uses of Literacy. Aspects of Working-Class Life with Special Reference to Publications and Entertainments*. He explained that, even in the 1950s, these girls enjoyed only a brief, flowery period. Between the time they left school and their marriage, they had just a few years in which they could please themselves and in which they could relish the prospect of spending money for their own pleasure and not for the benefit of others. For, as Booth stated, nearly all factory girls were destined to become mothers, but the fact of their motherhood did not necessarily mean an end to their industrial employment.

Clementina Black was of the opinion that four types of married women could be distinguished amongst the working class, and these she designated Classes A, B, C and D. The two former embraced the poor, and the two latter the upper working class, the married women of which were described collectively as a body of intelligent, able and efficient mothers. No country in the world could hope to have better citizens and it was further maintained that they were the bulwark of national prosperity, as much in the moral as in the material sense of the word. Class C was found to be particularly worthy of praise, with Black believing that the Women's Co-operative Guild largely represented this group. Most were overwhelmingly in favour of the issues which were dear to the hearts of middle-class activists like Black – women's suffrage and easier divorce. In comparison, though they were usually conspicuous by their competence and independence of mind, the women of Class D were depicted as reprehensible because, unlike those of Class C, they worked after marriage. Normally married to highly-skilled, well-paid husbands, they saw no wrong in their own paid employment, the income from which enabled their children to enjoy 'health giving holiday outings'. It also allowed the expansion of the educational opportunities open to their young; children could stay on at school because the wages of the mother meant that their earnings were not essential.

Despite the economic advantages conferred on a family by the added income of a working wife, the number of Class D women who chose to work was not high. Increasingly, the later years of the nineteenth century had seen a demarcation arise in the lives of the women of the upper working class: that life before they married and in which they worked for their own income, and that after marriage, when they became based at home and more reliant on their husband for money. It became a matter of respectability that a married woman relinquish paid employment – other than that which was associated with femininity and could be carried out in the home. Indeed, it was not until the First World War that this trend began to be reversed. Booth had recognised this phenomenon in London in the 1880s. As a rule, he found that the wives of artisans and most other regular wage-earners did not work, whilst the women of 'higher labour' also abandoned employment on marriage, except if they kept a shop or employed girls at laundry or dressmaking. In a book edited by J. Ramsay Macdonald in 1904 and entitled *Women in the Printing Trades. A Sociological Study*, it was deemed curious to

notice how few married women worked in Birmingham's
printing trade compared, for example, with the city's pen trade.
The curiosity was easily explained because it appeared that a
better class of girl coming from a better home entered the former
occupation, in contrast to the women employed in the hardware
trades. It was declared that it was very exceptional for a girl
who married a skilled artisan in Birmingham to continue her
work, and several employers in the city refused to engage
married women. The same effect was seen in Liverpool in 1912. It
was reported in *Social Conditions in Provincial Towns*, edited by
Helen Bosanquet, that it was unusual for the more respectable
working-class women to go to the factories after marriage,
although in certain lower-class industries the proportion of
married women was large.

These married working women of the poor, whom Black
regarded as the most overworked, the hardest pressed and
probably the unhappiest of working-class women, belonged to
her Class B. As mothers they were mostly concerned with the
future of their children and their present healthy support. It was
to help facilitate these objectives that they sought work, the
income from which would supplement their husbands' usually
inadequate and often irregular earnings. In taking this course
of action they provided a generally superior contrast to the
married women of Class A who, whilst their husbands' incomes
were also insufficient to meet the needs of their families, did not
go out to work. Included in this category were large numbers of
women who, for a variety of reasons, were helpless, incompetent
or in poor health and thus could not work. Furthermore, it
became apparent that, of the 'active' married women of the
urban poor, a significantly high proportion were in employment
during their married lives. Official figures tended to obscure
this fact, understating their numbers because of the often
infrequent, interrupted or part-time nature of their work. A
census provided for posterity figures applicable to one day, not
those relevant over a period of years. The census of 1901
exemplified this. It recorded the proportion of married women
who were at work in specified occupations in the whole of
Birmingham as nineteen per cent. Dr Robertson's survey, based
on information gathered from two of the city's poorest wards,
showed that out of 1,212 mothers included as statistical

evidence and who had borne children during 1908, 50·4% had worked during the year. It was concluded, therefore, that in the lower-working-class neighbourhoods of Birmingham, at least fifty per cent of married women worked in any year. Of the 611 mothers who were industrially employed, a staggering 70·5% chose to work in factories and workshops, compared to 20·5% who worked at home and nine per cent elsewhere. In spite of the fact that a woman's labour was usually cheap, employment in a factory did offer higher earnings than did other kinds of work: an average of 10s 1d a week in contrast to the average 4s 7d a week income of a married woman who was casually employed. In London, too, the extent to which women were wage-earners was not generally realised. Arthur Sherwell, in *Life in West London: A Study and a Contrast* (published in 1897), quoted figures relating to the dress trades of that city. Of the 82,000 heads of families engaged in that industry, no less than 30,000 were females. This proportion became even more striking if it was remembered that in cases where women kept their husbands, the man was still returned as the head of family.

The desirability or otherwise of so many married women of the urban poor working became a matter of much debate. Helen Bosanquet was of the strongly expressed opinion that where wives had children it was an 'unmitigated evil' for them to go to work. This action would inevitably lead to neglected homes, ailing children, and a wasteful expenditure of the money that was earned. In the textile districts it was common for husband and wife to work together and she believed nothing could so well emphasise the importance of the woman in the family as did the miserable conditions of the home and children which existed when the woman was at the mill. Booth also perceived a moral danger posed by the fact of married women working. He felt that no respectable man would willingly let the mother of his children go out to a factory, and that the ten shillings a week that she could earn could not make up for the loss incurred by her absence, even if the man's earnings were as little as eighteen shillings a week. Married women who did go out to work were, in his view, generally victims of a marital influence which had brutalised and degraded them. It was to be a recurring theme that it was the rougher and less skilled girls who married loafers, men who preferred to live off the earnings of their wives

rather than their own. The article 'Wives in a slum', in the study
edited by Black, echoed this assumption, the writer stating that,
in nearly all the families living in the district described, the
woman worked to keep the man who became, as a result, lazy
and a drifter. Cadbury and his associates were also of the
opinion that where a woman went out to work, the habits of her
husband deteriorated because the burden of responsibility for
the family was removed from him. It was further held by some
observers that not only did the character of the husband suffer
when his wife went out to work, so too did that of single girls
working in the same factory shop. The mischievous, lewd and
lascivious talk of married women could only lower the moral
standards of the young and unmarried. In contrast to the high
moral tone adopted by middle-class writers who castigated the
married working woman, the argument against their employment made by Ada Nield Chew was more practical; women who
had husbands at work should not be allowed to take the means
of subsistence away from girls who were dependent for their
livelihoods on their earnings.

Opposition to these statements was provided by some middle-
class feminists who, rightly in many respects, saw the married
working women of the urban poor as being in the vanguard of
the movement fighting for female freedom from male control.
For B. L. Hutchins in *Women in Modern Industry* (published in
1915), this was particularly the case. By the earning of her own
living and the control of her own wages, no matter how small,
she thought these women were, in reality, socially in advance of
middle- and upper-class women who, in an economic sense, were
still so often parasites. It was true that, through working for
their own money, many women of the urban poor enjoyed a
sense of freedom, no matter how limited this was by the
knowledge that each week their earnings were usually 'spoken
for' before they received them. One old woman who had worked
in a factory for sixty years was quoted by Cadbury as expressing
the opinion that a shilling she earned herself was worth two
given her by her husband. Nevertheless, it is important to be
aware that most women of the urban poor did not seek
employment because they were bored at home, or as the result of
a wish to exert their individuality and achieve their independence. These social effects came as a result of economic necessity

demanding that they earn money with which to boost the family budget, rather than through the conscious determination of married women. Even Booth admitted that whenever he had found women working for very low rates of pay, they had been forced into accepting that employment so as to earn a living for themselves and their children. In all his examples, the husbands were disabled or out of work. The Birmingham survey gave statistical evidence to justify this assertion. Of the 611 mothers included who were industrially employed, fifteen per cent had a husband who was unemployed, whilst only seventy of the women expressed a preference for that kind of work. Significantly, eighty-one mothers were the sole or main source of income of their families whilst the great majority, 556, went out to work so as to supplement the family income. A report in 1904 had stated that in Birmingham the average wage for an unskilled labourer was between seventeen shillings and twenty-one shillings a week. It was believed impossible on these figures to maintain a family of five other than in poverty, even assuming no expenditure by the husband on drink, tobacco and travel to and from work. There existed only two ways in which the family's income could be significantly increased if the children were young: by the taking in of lodgers or by the earnings provided by a working wife. The survey of 1908 emphasised these findings: in those homes where a mother did not work the average family income was 23s 1d a week compared with 20s 1d where the wife did work. Even the small amount a woman was able to earn could tide a family over a period of great poverty, and this was as true for the rest of the country as it was for Birmingham. B. L. Hutchins also contributed to Black's study. In Yorkshire she found that, of ninety-five working wives questioned, 63·2% stated that their employment was as a result of the insufficiency of the income provided by their husbands, whilst 30·57% gave other reasons of economic necessity. W. Wilkins reported in the same book that in Manchester only nineteen women from a sample of 120 explained their employment in any other way.

Large numbers of married women of the urban poor worked not because they particularly wished to, nor because they adhered fervently to the ideals of middle-class feminists, but because they had to. The argument that home and children suffered as a consequence of that employment was, in the case of most wives, erroneous. It was also a widely-held belief that a major cause of the high infant mortality rates in lower-working-class neighbourhoods was the precipitous return to work of many mothers after childbirth. Employment made it more difficult for a mother to breast-feed her baby and breast-feeding was an important influence in reducing the infant mortality rate. Of the 1908 Birmingham sample, only twenty-seven per cent of women who returned to work breast-fed their babies, compared with seventy-five per cent of those who did not work. Yet the married working women of the city had been shown as usually belonging to the poorest families which, without a mother's additional income, would undoubtedly have fallen deeper into a poverty that threatened life. A mother who breast-fed her baby found it difficult to work and thus lost wages which staved off the worst effects of poverty; a mother who returned to work could rarely breast-feed (although some had their babies brought to the factory for that purpose) and thus an infant was denied the nutrition that could be provided by the mother. The two cancelled each other out, especially when it was realised that, through a loss of her earnings, a woman who remained at home to breast-feed her infant could not feed herself, and thus her child, properly.

In the final analysis, it was poverty which affected a baby's health, not the manner of its feeding. This was expressively shown when the average weight of a twelve-month-old infant was related to a father's income: where this was under ten shillings a week the weight averaged 16·8 lb; where the income was between ten shillings and twenty shillings this was 17·5 lb, rising to 18·3 lb where the father earned between twenty shillings and thirty shillings and to 18·9 lb when that figure was over thirty shillings. A later report in 1914 emphasised the relevance of a father's income to the health of his children. It was revealed that, while the infantile death rate for children whose mother worked was only ten per 1,000 higher than that for those children whose mothers did not work, where fathers earned less than a pound a week, the rate was sixty-five per 1,000 higher than in the case of children whose fathers earned more than a pound. Of the children who survived their first year, sixty-five per cent of those from the latter group were in good health, compared to only fifty-three per cent of the former. Indeed, it was found that in the homes of the very poor a slightly higher percentage of children twelve months' old were in good health where their mothers worked. In contrast, in better-off families a child was healthier if a mother did not go out to work. Dr Duncan found much to praise in the married working women of the poor. Compared with those who did not work, whom she described in 1911 as indolent, lazy and inattentive to the needs of their children and homes, they were thrifty and energetic. Tens of thousands of families throughout England were undoubtedly kept from absolute want, squalor and misery by the labours of dedicated mothers at home and at work. Despair was not the characteristic of the married working woman; rather she was distinguished by her fortitude and devotion to duty in providing as comfortable a life as possible for her family. The heroism of these women was singular, their hard work spectacular. A woman from Birmingham remembered with wonderment how her own mother coped with the problems posed by poverty:

'Cus I think it's only really in later years women aint really been the underdogs. Mom was the most important. Her was always there and her was always working in the house. However her managed I don't know. It was only as I got older ... I did wonder ... But her used to go to work. Her worked at Shelley's at nights and when we was kids her always had home-work, radiators from Beaumonts. These used to be a big brass rod and used to have to thread some square and some round on it ... And we all used to help daytime and nightime ... Cleaning as well at a pub ... of a morning. Hard working woman. All the housework. And such as the grandkids, if they wanted anythink washed and ironed for a dance.[21]

Night work, especially during the 1920s and 1930s, enabled a woman to work at a factory and still be at home during the day. Snatching sleep whenever she could, a mother in this position could not only cook and clean for her family, she could also take on other part-time work. The cost to her health was obviously great, yet if her children were better provided for by dint of her exertions, then a mother thought her toil and weakened constitution was worthwhile. 'Home work' or 'out work' offered a readily acceptable alternative to the factory for women with large families. The work was obviously carried out at home, where its pace was dictated by the woman and all the other

numerous demands made on her time. Freed from the routine of
factory work, a mother could adapt this employment to her
duties as mother and housewife, whilst her children might be
able to help her. However, home work was usually monotonous,
invariably arduous and always low-paid. Arthur Harding's
mother made matchboxes for Bryant and May for a period. She
was able to make eight gross a day, for which she was paid 1s 6d,
2¼d a gross, and her toil left her 'fagged out' by the end of each
day's work. On another occasion she started making coal sacks,
which Harding described as hard work, unsuitable for a woman,
especially if she was undernourished. Helen Bosanquet was of
the opinion that home work was inevitably accompanied by
dirt, disorder and badly-cared-for children. Few women, however, would have been attracted to the industries connected
with this kind of employment if they had not needed the extra
income it provided for their family's better comfort. Cadbury
found that only 0.4% of women worked at such tasks for 'pocket
money', the great majority doing so to supplement their
husband's wages which were either too small or too irregular, or
because – in the case of forty-six per cent – they were widows or
deserted wives. Dirt and disorder there may have been, but the
charge of badly-neglected children was a slur on the care for
their chldren's welfare which women engaged in home work
always had uppermost in their minds. When George Acorn's
father was taken off to hospital, where he remained for nine
months, his mother reassured her husband, with a fierce, almost
tigrish look, that she would become father and mother to their
children. Each day she worked until after midnight making
boxes. Acorn had little doubt that she was often ill from the
damp, paste-smelling atmosphere which pervaded their home,
but she never complained.

In 1901 a Factories and Workshop Act empowered sanitary
authorities to prohibit certain kinds of home work, for example
tailoring, upholstery and electro-plating, so long as the occupation was likely to be dangerous on account of overcrowding or
bad ventilation or posed a danger to the health of others owing
to the presence of infectious disease. Additionally, a factory
owner who made use of home workers could be required to send
a list of those he employed in this manner to the local Medical
Officer of Health. A visit was then to be made to these homes if

possible. What the Act did not affect was wages and these remained chronically low. The Reverend T. J. Bass recorded those relating to a number of 'classic' sweated industries in Birmingham. A button-sewer, who had to buy her own cotton, could earn between eightpence and one shilling for an eight-hour day if she sewed on twenty gross; that is, 2,880 buttons. The sewing on of hooks and eyes, often by candlelight, was a particularly monotonous and ill-paid task, with the card on which they were sewn passing through the worker's hands three times: first to stitch on the eye; second to link the hook to the eye, and finally to stitch on the hook. A 'clever' worker could earn the pittance of 1s 6d a week, after 1¼d had been deducted for a reel of cotton provided by an employer. For gluing 144 boxes, the same number of lids and a gross of labels onto the boxes, a woman might earn between fourpence and 1s 6d, depending on the type of box concerned. In the Black Country many women worked at the particularly strenuous task of chainmaking. The work could be carried on in a shed behind a woman's home, or in one used by five or six women. Robert Sherard described the living and working conditions of the chainmakers of Cradley Heath. He recounted how one woman carried out her task whilst also caring for her baby. A pole ran across the shed from which dangled a tiny swing chair. The infant was seated in this so that the mother might rock the child as she worked. In a week of hard labour the husband and wife, working together, could make a ton of spikes for which they earned twenty shillings. Out of this they paid 3s 8d for fuel, the same sum for the rent of the house and workshop and one shilling for the hire of their tools, which left them with 11s 8d a week to provide for all the other needs of their family. Chainmakers were paid 5s 4d a hundred-weight for heavy chain. If a woman was lucky she might be able to make 1½ cwt in a week. Only an intense loyalty to her children could have induced a mother to struggle at a job like this. It is true that the poverty of these families could have been relieved by their entering the workhouse, but the success of poorly-paid women of the lower working class is revealed in their willing-ness to take on any task which might yet feed their families and maintain their unity and independence. The haggard, worn and tired faces of the working women of the urban poor are to be seen in this light; they were the signs of victory not of failure.

In many industrial cities and centres the opportunity did not exist for women to work in factories as it did in Birmingham, London or Salford. For example, in Middlesbrough iron-working was virtually the only industry and this offered no employment for women. Lady Bell believed that because there was no organised women's labour the women of the town had no independent existence of their own. However, here as elsewhere in the country a woman did not have to rely on factory or home work to earn her own money. Numerous ways existed in which she could support herself or increase the family's housekeeping. Some of these offered as little remuneration as did 'sweated' home work, yet it was still a necessary and vital infusion of funds. This kind of 'irregular' work carried on by married women also exhibited a kind of class structure. Cadbury considered that hawking salt was the only activity more wretched than hawking firewood and that those women involved in both could almost be called part of the 'submerged'. The same view was stated in Black's study, women wood-choppers being regarded as constituting a rough group of a low social grade. The earnings from both occupations were small: salt could be bought off a coal barge for twopence a lump, which was then cut up into four pieces and sold for a penny a piece. A woman did well to earn threepence a day. Old orange and bacon boxes could be bought for fourpence and, chopped up into firewood, sold for sixpence. In London wood-bundlers earned roughly threepence per hundred and could achieve this in an hour, depending on the nature of the wood, making at the most two shillings a day. Wood-choppers, too, earned threepence per hundred. Robert Roberts could recall that in Salford elderly women, broken like horses, could be hired for threepence to drag a hundredweight of coke in a wagon for a mile or so. Some might see in them an ultimate degradation of spirit; instead it exemplified the unquenching spirit and dogged determination of the women of the urban poor to remain free and in control of their own lives. Rag-sorting and waste-paper-sorting were other low-status means of earning a living. Those engaged in this latter occupation earned two shillings per hundredweight for good, clean paper and fourpence per hundredweight for brown and dirty paper. After allowing for the hire of a barrow – plenty of walking was involved in this occupation – perhaps a shilling a day could be earned. Another means of employment was more macabre. George Acorn recalled women in London making a living from washing the bodies of the dead. The evidence provided in Chapter one, regarding the duties of matriarchs, would suggest that payment for this practice was not common.

Superior to these largely outdoor tasks came those which Cadbury regarded as the second type of home work. As opposed to trade work, this was that kind of employment which could be regarded as an extension of domestic work. The taking in of washing and charring – the cleaning of another woman's house – were the two main activities in this area. As with industrial home work, these activities appealed to a certain type of woman, and for the same kind of reasons. In general, it was the older woman who had a large family and needed some control over the time and pace of her work who was engaged in these tasks. Indeed, in Birmingham, on average, her family would be twice as large as that of a woman who worked in a factory. Both occupations, too, manifested the ill-effects of industrial home work in that they were substantially unskilled, usually strenuous and always poorly-paid. They were also plagued by competition. This latter problem was made explicit with regard to charring in the work edited by Clementina Black. Charwomen were likely to have to resort to their work because they were either widows or were the wives of husbands who were in irregular or low-paid employment. Given that in the late-Victorian and Edwardian eras these determinants of poverty were widespread, the result was that there were more charladies available than there was work. This difficulty was exacerbated by the influx into their ranks of those who saw charring as a temporary means to alleviate distress brought on by strikes or seasonal unemployment.

Charring, like other forms of employment, also exhibited a hierarchy of status reflected by the social standing of the families for whom a charlady cleaned. Yet, whatever the grade of their jobs, all charladies were characterised by the fact that they were women of the urban poor who performed the rough and arduous tasks eschewed by the better-off of society. A regular day's work, starting at 9 a.m. and finishing at 3 p.m., consisted of washing and drying up the breakfast dishes; filling up the coal scuttles from the out-house; cleaning the fire irons

with emery cloth; blackleading the fire-grate; dusting, cleaning
and polishing cutlery and ornaments, and beating and shaking
the carpets outside. For a woman who was regularly employed
in charring and who enjoyed a good reputation amongst those
who employed her as one who was reliable, trustworthy and
diligent, then benefits in kind were added to her pay:

Our Gran used to have to get up at 4 o'clock every morning . . . and
she'd do a lot of washing and then she'd go to the laundry. Work again.
Then she'd come home, do her home work – got to look arter the kids.
When she had all the children coming along, she had to tek daily jobs
on. She used to work for somebody up Runcorn Road, a posh road then
and they was all gaffers, you know, masters. Our Gran always used to
call 'em, 'yes 'm' and 'master' and all this, that and the other . . . and
sometimes Gran used to like to work at night and they used to have
parties . . . 'Cus she used to wait at the table and then what was left she
used to bring for her children.[22]

This oral evidence from Birmingham referred to the early
1890s. By the turn of the century, the use of the term 'master' had
fallen into abeyance except amongst some of the old.

It is important to be aware that where domestic service was
unpopular amongst the women of the urban poor, charring,
which was similar in many respects, was not. Yet, despite a
superficial similarity, there existed vital differences. A charlady was more independent, she maintained her own home and
could terminate her employment more easily if she wished,
especially if her husband's earnings increased or if other part-
time employment offered itself. Most of the teenage girls
amongst the poor were prejudiced against domestic service
because it entailed 'living-in' with the employer, at whose beck
and call a lowly general servant always seemed to be. This
position was also an isolated one, cut off from others of a similar
station in society. As early as 1890 the Registry Offices and
Training Homes (which supplied an employer with servants)
had observed that the combination of greater freedom and
comradeship was leading to a marked disinclination in the
women of the urban poor to become domestic servants. Instead
they preferred factory work, even if it was at starvation wages.
One type of employment which could roughly be included under
the heading of domestic service did remain popular; that of a
bar-maid. The hours were long and the pay poor, ten shillings for
a ninety-hour week, from which sum was deducted breakages. It

also meant living in. Yet, for a certain type of girl of the urban poor, it was attractive. If she was an orphan or estranged from her parents, work in a pub offered not only employment but also a home. In addition she was not isolated socially as was a servant employed in a middle- or upper-class home; her work meant that she was meeting people and many barmaids courted their future husbands across the bar of a public house.

Extended domestic service work embraced a variety of other activities similar in their nature to charring. By blackleading the grates of the more prosperous of the working class, a woman could earn between six and seven shillings a week in Birmingham around 1900. Wyn Heywood regularly distempered the kitchens of similar families so as to earn enough money to enable her to pay the rent, and Catherine Cookson's mother hung paper, painted ceilings and even replaced window frames for three shillings a day. Other women earned money by caring for the children of mothers who worked at regular jobs in the factory or laundry. It must be noted here, however, that the extent to which this prevailed was often exaggerated by those of the middle class who wished to maximise the dangers, as they saw it, of mothers working. A vital part of their argument was that the young infants of these women were left in the care of other children or neighbours who were unable to, or did not wish to, render the infants the care necessary for their physical and moral well-being. This was contradicted by a report from Birmingham which showed the extent to which mothers who worked sought also to make sure that their children were looked after in the best manner possible during their absence. Their actions also emphasised once more the communal self-help of the poor and the importance of older women and matriarchs. In the report of 1906, Dr Robertson revealed that out of 771 cases inquired into of mothers who went out to work whilst their infants were under twelve months, the following provisions were made for the children: 396 babies were cared for by a neighbour; 267 were looked after in their own home by an adult, usually a grandmother or other relative; 100 were taken to the home of a relative living in a neighbouring home, whilst in only seven instances were the children looked after by youngsters under the age of twelve, and in one case the baby was put in the charge of a day nursery. These findings verified those of another study which were quoted in the book by Jill Liddington and Jill Norris. The Women's Co-operative Guild was particularly concerned about child care, and one of their members in Burnley, a Mrs Ashworth, organised a local survey into the care of children whose mothers worked. The results, published in 1894 in *The Labour Gazette*, showed that out of 165 children involved, one in four were left with grandparents; a further one in four were in the charge of relatives; nearly half were minded by neighbours, and in only nine instances were the children left with no-one to take care of them.

In the practice of child-minding, the neighbourhood support networks established by the women of the urban poor themselves are very much in evidence. Many relatives and neighbours provided the service of child-minding as part of their adherence to the concept of 'good neighbourliness'. Naturally, this act entailed a certain reciprocity of duty on behalf of the mother who was gaining financially because another allowed her the freedom to return to work. Recompense would be offered, but it was often little more than the few shillings necessary to feed the baby; for example, Kathleen Dayuss's mother minded her infant son so that she could work in a factory. Her mother did not gain financially from this arrangement, for the five shillings a week which Dayuss paid her were spent on rusks and milk for the child. In certain circumstances, however, relatives or neighbours might be desperately in need of an income and this could be provided by child-minding. This was often the case with older, widowed women who were struggling to maintain their independence and who were striving to remain out of the workhouse. Minding the children of relatives and neighbours for a fee enabled them to do this. The ignorant and careless professional child-minder was not as widespread in poor neighbourhoods as it might have been thought. Instead, both the child-minders and those women who placed their children in their care were engaging in an expressive example of neighbourliness.

Child-minding was an example of 'penny capitalism', as was the taking in of washing. This phenomenon has been studied by John Benson in *The Penny Capitalists. A Study of Nineteenth Century Working Class Entrepreneurs*, and he argued that the term excluded outworkers, the self-employed and sub-contractors. Instead, he defined penny capitalists as working-class people who were operating on a small scale and who were prepared to assume risks in the hope of making a profit. They were also distinguished by a variety of responsibilities: they were in charge of the whole process, however small; they had to acquire the necessary capital, choose a site, and bargain for raw materials; they had to decide their working methods and provide the tools, and they had to find a market for the finished product. Elizabeth Roberts found that, in the three towns she studied, between forty per cent and forty-two per cent of working-class mothers were involved in some form of penny-capitalist activity after their marriage. She believed that the resultant addition to the income of families helped to explain the paradox of a healthier-than-average population existing on earnings on or below the poverty line. As we have seen, the urban poor, as opposed to the working class as a whole, were very often under-nourished, but I have little doubt that this argument has its implications for the health of that section. For, without the money earned by wives and mothers who were engaged in penny-capitalist activity of some kind, the lower working class of England must have become even more underfed, with all the deleterious effects to their health that this would have had.

Some forms of penny-capitalist activity were not applicable to the urban poor. For example, the selling of home-made food or drink was only realistic from a house which possessed two rooms downstairs, and few impoverished families could boast that. Lodging, too, was rarer, given the over crowded conditions of many lower-working-class homes, although it was a feasible proposition for old people, spinsters and those with few or no children. However, the most common form of penny-capitalist activity for women who dwelt in the slums was the taking in of washing. This was usually part-time in its nature and was determined, as was charring, by the inadequate income of a family. Indeed, as John Benson has said, part-time penny capitalism was a defensive action which attempted to combat the immediate financial needs of a family, although, of course, these needs might continue unabated for many years. It was also typically the resort of women, unlike full-time penny-capitalist activity which was dominated by middle-aged, skilled males. That is not to say that part-time capitalists, even amongst the poor, could not become full-time. An example was provided in the Studley Street locality by a woman who took in washing and who eventually became the proprietor of a high-class laundry in the street. Women such as this were obviously distinguished by their rarity and the usual resort of women who took in washing and who wished to work full-time was employment in a laundry.

The 1901 census showed that, with charring, employment in a laundry was one of only two women's occupations in which unmarried women were in the minority. It was also a sweated industry which was not brought under the supervision of Trades Boards until 1919, and – not surprisingly – laundries were mostly situated in poverty-stricken neighbourhoods in which cheap labour was readily available. Throughout the Victorian era, wages paid to washers in full-time work were between two shillings and 2s 6d a day. This made laundresses at the turn of the century a very poorly-paid group of workers, especially when it is realised that much full-time laundry work was seasonal and episodic, particularly in London. However, these wages were still higher than those paid to washer women in private homes which averaged between one shilling and 1s 6d a day, with food provided. Figures paid to women who took in washing and who accomplished the task in their own homes are harder to come across and they probably varied from town to town according to the kind of washing a woman took in. However, John Benson believed that, around 1900, as a rule women were paid 2s 6d to wash and iron a bundle of washing. A Birmingham woman remembered that in the 1920s a local church choir paid her mother eighteen pence a dozen to wash, starch and iron its surpluses. This kind of work obviously required a certain skill but was still not well-paid, and it would appear likely that wages in general were depressed by the need of washerwomen to find work at any price. This observation would seem to be confirmed by a comment from *The Pall Mall Gazette*, which was quoted by Patricia Malcolmsen in *English Laundresses. A Social History 1850–1930*. The correspondent in question declared that 'widows and washing, misery and mayhem' seemed, somehow, indissolubly connected.

Washing was an occupation replete with its own terminology. In Birmingham it would be carried out in 'the brew'us', a colloquial term for the outbuilding of a terrace of back-to-backs in which the coppers were found. These were receptacles, set in brick, which were capable of holding about twenty gallons of water. They were filled up by the bucketful from a sink in the brewhouse, after which a fire would be lighted in a small compartment beneath the copper so that the water – to which had been added 'Pretty Polly', a form of washing powder – could be boiled. Once this had happened, the water was transferred to tubs in which the actual washing was accomplished. The labour involved in this process was very great and it necessitated a substantial degree of physical strength in women. Patricia Malcolmsen gave one estimate regarding the amount of water a washerwoman, or laundress, would use in her task. For a simplified laundry process which included a single wash of one period of boiling and rinsing, it was estimated that fifty gallons of water would be moved in tubs which held five to six gallons each.

In Birmingham these tubs were provided by sawing beer barrels – sold by local breweries for two shillings each in the 1930s – into two parts, one larger and one smaller. Once the water had been boiled, the larger tub, known as the 'maiding tub', was filled. Maiding was the process whereby the washing was 'thumped' clean. To achieve this a 'dolly' was used. This was a four- or five-legged stool attached to an upright handle across which there was a crossbar handle. In Birmingham the stool was replaced by a block of wood, indented at intervals, which was properly called a laundry punch; in the North-East it was replaced by a perforated copper cone known locally as a 'possing stick'. Once maided, the washing would be transferred to the smaller of the two tubs and scrubbed using a scrubbing board. It was then swilled and the 'whites' were transferred into the copper where they were boiled using fresh water. After this they were swilled for the last time by dipping them into a bucket of water into which a cube of 'Reckitt's blue' had been hung. This gave the clothes a 'blue-whiteness' much admired by the poor (and which is still popular). Following this, the washing which had to be starched, such as table-cloths, pillows and shirts, was put to one side and dipped into a bucket in which the starch had been made up. The whites would then be mangled and pegged out to dry with the 'coloureds' (which had not been boiled). Finally, the boiling hot water left in the copper would but put into buckets and bowls. In some of these, overalls and other heavily-stained clothing and linen would be soaked, whilst the rest would be used to clean the brewhouse and the staircases in the house.

Catherine Cookson recalled that for days on end, week in, week out, year in, year out, the kitchen of her home would be hung with damp washing. This so affected her that she always hated the sight of lines full of washing. This feeling is reflected in my oral evidence from Birmingham, several women expressing the opinion that they hated wash day because of the way the washing, as it dried, seemed to fill every part of the house, especially in bad weather. Although rhymes exist which extol the virtue of women who washed early in the week, many women had no choice as to the day of this labour. In Birmingham the older residents, often matriarchs, had the pick of the days, whilst working wives and those who took in washing for a living had to wash by the light of a candle or at weekends. Once the washing had dried, the final task was to iron and fold it and then, of course, to return it to its owner for payment. Washing was taken in for anybody who could pay for it and – as one Birmingham man believed – who was too lazy to do it herself. Teachers would often ask a mother, or mothers, of a large family to wash for them. Not only were they saved the hard work that washing entailed, but they were also providing a vital source of income to families who were hard-pressed financially. This was a very local activity in which concerned members of the middle class helped those of the poor who helped themselves.

Before a woman was able to take in washing and thus supplement her housekeeping money, it was necessary that she possess a mangle, that essential prerequisite of her occupation. In the Edwardian era these could be bought for between four and five pounds each second-hand, although they were double that price new. In the former case, this was the equivalent of at least four to five weeks' wages for a skilled man, which meant that it was unrealistic for a woman of the urban poor to expect to buy one for cash. However, so long as she knew that she would be able to attract customers, options were available to her which enabled her to purchase a mangle. She might pawn whatever she could, especially her wedding ring, to raise the money she needed; she might buy one off a 'club' man or from a shop which sold articles on a form of hire purchase, or she might borrow the cash she needed from a money-lender. All these ways incurred a debt, but one that was necessary if a woman was to earn money, and of course they hoped that their earnings would quickly clear their debt. Interestingly, the purchase of a mangle could also be a form of neighbourhood help. Elizabeth Roberts revealed that in Preston, before 1914, it was the practice for the neighbours of a woman who was recently widowed, and who was the mother of a large family, to help her to support herself by making a collection so that she might buy a mangle and thus take in washing. In other parts of the country, women who did not have a mangle were not necessarily precluded from this occupation. Arthur Harding remembered that their dilemma was solved in his neighbourhood by a woman who charged those less fortunate than her around a penny a dozen articles for the use of her mangle.

At the pinnacle of irregular and extended domestic work came a form of part-time penny-capitalist activity not mentioned by John Benson. This was that of women who dealt in second-hand clothes, known generally by the euphemism of 'wardrobe dealers'. George Gissing mentioned one in *The Nether World*. The character Mrs Todd had recently been widowed and she supported herself and her four children by selling second-hand children's clothes from a stall. Wardrobe dealers, readily noticed by their habit of carrying large black bags into which they put their acquisitions, called on homes in middle-class areas in the hope of buying, or being given, any clothes the occupants wished to dispose of. At home these would be patched and mended, if needed, and then a 'pitch' would be hired at a market from where they would be sold. In Birmingham, the most popular was the Rag Market by the Bull Ring. As the son of one wardrobe dealer recollected, before 1914:

Used to pay about a shilling for the afternoon to the toll keeper, to do business there . . . Get your stuff out of the trolley and lay it out on the floor, doing your best to encourage the people to buy the stuff . . . And if you'd got anything about you, if you was a typical Brummie and knowed your way about the place, you could mek yourself a bob or two out of it . . . Our old lady had the gift of the gab. She'd see two women come along, she'd gie 'em the gee, you know, to encourage them. And 'er used to go,
"Ee 'are, ma wench! 'Ave a look at this lot! What about this lot!'

She'd hold up a pair of bloomers, you know all open down the front they used to be. Only two pieces where they put their leg through, see? And they used to call 'em 'Ever-ready's' or 'Free-traders'. And the old girl used to pick 'em up,
"Ee 'are, ma wench, how'll these do you? How much? Ar. Fourpence to you. Alright.'
And they'd wrap 'em up and tek 'em away.[23]

The ambition of most wardrobe dealers was to graduate to running their own second-hand clothes shop in their own neighbourhood. This was achieved by this mother.

Without doubt the earning of her own money increased a woman's self-sufficiency. This was very important to survival in a poverty-stricken neighbourhood. The numerous examples of women who worked to earn a living for their families after the death, illness or injury of their husbands only emphasise this fact. Without women like these, the workhouses would have been insufficient to cater for the vast numbers of destitute poor, and a tremendous burden would have been added to a nation which was inadequately prepared to deal with the problems of poverty. It therefore redounded on the poor, most particularly the women of the urban poor, to cope with the almost insurmountable difficulties of slum life. The successful woman was just one of hundreds of thousands like her who developed attributes which were not needed by women belonging to other sections of society. Her triumph was gained at the expense of femininity in favour of physical and mental strength and an independence of body and spirit. If poverty could not defeat these women, then neither could middle-class men impose their masculine concepts of womanhood on them, and nor could their husbands dominate them. Lower-working-class women may have lived in a society that was openly patriarchal in a decided fashion, but if they did so it was only because they chose it to be that way. That choice was made possible by the independence their own earnings gave them, as well as by their control of the family's finances. This allowed many women the confidence to leave a man the semblance of power whilst they, in reality, controlled the family. Financial independence was vital if a woman was not to become a serf, tied not to the land but to her home. Moreover, freedom of action and unrestricted movement could only take place in a society which gave women the opportunity to support themselves.

It was supposed by many commentators that the women of the working class led generally uninteresting and boring lives. Their worlds were regarded as claustrophobically small, largely limited by the four walls of their homes, outside which they ventured only to make purchases from the local corner shop. This was often the only place where a proper conversation could be carried on with other women. Roberts reported that in his mother's shop these conversations regularly took the form of a bitter complaint on the confinement of daily life. Some of the wives he knew managed an occasional visit to the cemetery, or stole an hour in a balding park at the edge of their village. Most, however, were denied even this occasional variation in their humdrum lives. He was aware of one woman who spoke wearily of never having been five minutes' walk from her home in the eighteen years she had been married. The boredom of this daily pattern of existence for many women and the uniformity of the scenery they witnessed was not always understood by their menfolk. As the eldest son of a family which lived just above the poverty line in Birmingham remembered, his mother 'hadn't used to go out'. He was of the opinion that she did not need to because she had enough to do in the house and, if she wished, she could always talk to the mothers who lived on either side of their home. Mrs Pember-Reeves witnessed the same state of affairs in Lambeth amongst families of a similar economic standing. Here women seldom bought new clothes and often went without boots simply because it was felt that a mother had no need to appear in the light of day and thus did not need to dress herself prettily or gaily.

Rowntree believed that no-one could fail to be struck by the monotony which characterised the lives of most married women of the working class. Nevertheless, he did observe a distinction in the degree of that monotony, feeling that it was least marked in the slum districts. With the advance of the social scale, he believed that family life became more private, with the women left in the house all day whilst their husbands went out to work. In fact, the only outside interest many wives from the upper working class had was in their membership of the Women's Co-operative Guild or of a religious club like the Mothers' Union, based at a parish church. Women of the lower working class spent their lives enclosed within the bounds of a narrow area in which they would often find their employment as well as their residence, if they worked. Nevertheless, within the limited confines of their locality they were not as restricted socially as were their more financially secure sisters, and again poverty acted as a catalyst for their relative freedom. The houses of the poor were small, their furnishings sparse and their comfort minimal. This in itself encouraged their women to spend whatever time they could on the street, which became as much a centre of community life for wives as it was for husbands or children. As a result, a spectacle common to poor neighbourhoods was that of apparently idle groups of wives passing the day in gossip with their neighbours. Apparently, because these groups were amoeba-like in their nature; one wife would join and another would leave shortly afterwards, so that the actual time any individual woman might spend as part of the group could be short. Furthermore, whilst a woman of the urban poor preferred to pass any spare time she had in chat with others, open to public view and reproach, the wives of the upper working class spent their moments of relaxation indoors and thus evaded the slur of idleness. The street was not the only space in which the poor woman might meet people other than her family. A courtyard also provided a place in which wives and mothers could congregate: children played in the yard; water was obtained from a standpipe centrally placed in it; communal lavatories situated in the yard had to be cleaned, and of course women met as they washed or 'pegged out'. Life for a lower-working-class woman did not necessarily have to be dull. Although it was certainly tiring and strenuous, it could be made bearable by a camaraderie shared with neighbours and enlivened with incidents provided by squabbling children or quarrels between, and amongst, families. This kind of incident was not absent from the roads of the better-off of the working class, but it was certainly rarer.

Margery Spring Rice's comment that those wives of the working class who were not employed led lives cut of from the world outside their homes, eating, sleeping and 'resting' on the scene of their solitary labour, was not normally applicable to the married women of the poor. Significantly though, work expanded the number of their contacts, allowed a variation in their topics of conversation and provided a vital means of escape from the home and all of the problems associated with it. This was particularly the case with factory employment, which though often repetitive and uninspiring was not carried on in the house as was home work. Whatever the kind of work and wherever it was carried on, it gave a woman an income of her own which was important for her self-esteem as well as contributing to the housekeeping. Of course, most weeks the greatest part of her earnings was spent on essentials for her family in general rather than on herself alone. Yet her wages remained just that – hers. They belonged to her, not to her husband, and it was up to the woman who worked to decide how to spend her income. That the vast majority chose to do so on their families is a tribute to their devotion rather than a sign of a lack of choice. Because a choice did exist. A mother could relinquish the responsibilities of motherhood and spend her earnings on pleasure whilst her children were neglected. Uncaring mothers were as noticeable in the slums as they were elsewhere in society, whilst the ideal of motherhood was not aspired to by all the women of the urban poor. A Birmingham man, born in 1932, remembered vividly how, in his early childhood, his young mother daily returned from the local public house drunk and smelling of beer. She also kept bottles of beer hidden around the home so that she could enjoy a drink outside opening hours. Her husband tried to limit her drinking by handling all the money himself but she began to borrow small sums off her children, their earnings from part-time jobs. Finally, in 1939 the mother left home, deserting her seven children – all aged under eleven – and went to live with a man whom she had met during her drinking sessions.

For the majority of wives, working or not, little was left from their wages or the pool of housekeeping money – which was equally regarded as theirs – by the end of the week. Yet if a few coppers remained after provision had been made for the family, then the poor saw little wrong in women spending this, their money, on themselves. Entertainment was not restricted in a lower-working-class neighbourhood. There was nearly always a 'flea-pit' (low-status cinema), often a small fairground established on waste land by a few travelling families, and usually a music hall nearby. Attempts were also made by the middle class to attract the women of the poor into character-forming clubs or meetings. These usually foundered through indifference and, as a result, drew most of their members from the better-off of the working class, although women's settlements were more successful than most in attracting lower-working-class wives to their activities. These would be established at a house in a poor area at which resident workers, supplemented by enthusiastic voluntary helpers, sought to provide help and advice for the women of the district. Their relative success was ensured because they offered social amenities and talks which were of immediate relevance in the battle against poverty. At the Birmingham Women's Settlement there were two women's evenings each week; a maternity club to which weekly payments were made to provide for the expenses of a confinement; a Mothers' Guild once a week, at which two doctors gave free consultations and advice on the feeding and general care of infants, and there was also a kindergarten and play and reading hours for young children. Talks for working men and women were given on subjects like the 'Children's Act', 'Our duties as citizens' and 'Domestic training for girls', and each Tuesday a representative from the Poor Man's Lawyer Association was available to give advice. Nevertheless, women's settlements were as didactic in their nature as were religious organisations, although seeking to instruct women in an image of womanhood more commensurate with the ideas of Clementina Black and B. L. Hutchins than those of Helen Bosanquet. Consequently, it was once again the 'respectable' of the poor and lower 'castes' of the upper working class who were more likely to be attracted to the facilities they offered. The majority of the women of the urban poor preferred to spend their free time and whatever money they had left to themselves in a less organised way, deciding for themselves what form it should take. For teenage girls, this usually meant a walk along the local 'monkey run' – a main thoroughfare in an area along which boys and girls would parade in order to meet each other, or if they were older, as Booth stated, in going to a music hall or a public house with their boyfriends. The latter also provided the main form of entertainment for older, married women.

In his authoritative book, *Drink and The Victorians. The Temperance Question in England, 1815–72*, Brian Harrison expressed the opinion that from the 1820s women were excluded from public houses. It is certainly true that the fact of women drinking became inextricably connected with middle-class notions of respectability, so much so that women from this class assiduously avoided licensed premises if they wished to remain respectable. So too did most women of the upper working class – although some wives from the lowest reaches of this section went out for a drink with their husbands on a Saturday night, at least in Birmingham. However, large numbers of the poor did not adhere to the standards of conduct regarded as acceptable by most of English society. Instead, they lived according to their own codes in which respectability was generally a term attributed to a person's character rather than their economic standing. Thus it was not a sign of 'roughness' in a woman if she drank in a public house, or more usually a beer house (these were more common in poor neighbourhoods and possessed a licence only to sell beer and not spirits). If drink provided a lower-working-class man with a cheap form of temporary escape from the worries that haunted him, if the beer house offered him a warm, friendly and alluring alternative to a cold and unattractive home, then the same could be as forcefully true for the married women of the urban poor. The brightness and 'mateyness' available in a beer house were as tempting for them as they were for their husbands, holding out a pleasant contrast to the dreary surroundings in which they passed their lives, as one Birmingham son of an Edwardian mother remembered:

Yes, she used to like a drink of a night time.
Sunday night it used to tek her about an hour, hour and a half to get spruced up, go up to the corner to have a pint ... Doing her hair out, you know, plaiting it and coconut oil on it to gie it a gloss ... coiling the plaits round the side of her head.
And her used to put her stays on and pull 'em tight, you know, to get a little bit of the size orf her ... But by the time she'd come back she'd had the stays on too tight, and she'd say,
    'Oh, get these stays orf!'
... All so's her could sit in the pub and look nice and shapely ... just to have a couple of halves with her neighbours.[24]

Kathleen Dayuss also recalled that weekend drinking for women, as for men, was 'ritualised' by an improvement in their appearance. On a Saturday night her mother wore a white starched pinafore, kept especially for this one night out, and she marched off for a drink with her husband, wearing his flat cap.

Not all women of the urban poor drank in beer houses. Some preferred to buy beer from its off-licence section – known as an 'outdoor' in Birmingham as in Salford – and drink it at home. Once there, the red-hot poker might often be taken out of the fire, scraped on the bars of the fire-grate and plunged into the jug which held the drink. The beer would hiss and steam and when the froth had been brought up, as Rose Golding recalled, it was then seen fit to drink. Equally, not all women drank alcohol and, very importantly, lower-working-class society helped set limits for those who did. It was not seen fit for a young, single woman to drink alone, or with others of her kind, in a public or beer house. If she did she was regarded as 'an old tail' or prostitute. Neither was it generally accepted, before the First World War, that a girl who was courting should accompany her boyfriend for a drink, despite Booth's observation to the contrary. Those women in whom drinking in a beer house was seen as acceptable behaviour were normally older, married women, although an occasional younger wife might join them. A familiar scene in licensed premises was of several of these wives sitting together shelling peas in readiness for their husbands' dinners, often accompanied by their children, until an Act in 1908 forbade their presence. In an important reflection on the freedom of action enjoyed by the older married women of the urban poor, as well as on their lack of dependence on their husbands, those who drank did so with other wives and did not sit with their menfolk. Mrs Liddel, the wife of a vicar, observed in *A Shepherd of the Sheep* that in Jarrow in the late 1870s some bars in the town's public houses were frequented entirely by women. This fact was as particularly noticeable in Birmingham. A woman from this city remembered that in the 1920s and 1930s the wives who drank in the local beer house:

used to be in the passage ... There used to be like a window where people could go and fetch the jug and that, the outdoor. They'd be standing in there talking about everyone ... They wouldn't go in the bar. I mean, if they did go in the bar – which they did at times – they wouldn't sit with their husbands, they'd sit on different tables. They'd never sit with their husbands like they do now.[25]

Roberts noticed the same occurrence in Salford, where the women also drank either in the outdoor or, if they were not 'overfaced', beshawled in the bar. In Birmingham the section of a bar where the women congregated together, away from their husbands, was distinguished by a title bestowed upon it by their menfolk: in the district of Sparkbrook it was known as the 'Duck Pen', in Aston as the 'Cow Shed'. In London too, as Ellen Ross has indicated, there was a considerable women's 'pub' culture. The evidence from London suggests that in that city some wives did drink with their husbands and it indicates another reason why women drank. A. P. Jasper's mother occasionally went for a drink and sat with her husband, simply because when he called for a round he would often forget his change, which the barman, who knew the family, would push over to his wife. A woman from Paddington recalled that, as her marriage wore on, her mother would go the pub because it was also the only way she could get any money out of her husband.

Most wives who drank could not afford to become drunk, the paucity of their spending money limiting the amount of beer they could consume. There were those, though, who were either unmindful mothers or else were buoyed by the income of working children and thus could spend more than most on their pleasure. There were also those on whom year after year of hardship had taken its toll and who therefore sought solace in over-drinking. Grace Foakes did not like to see a woman drunk, although this happened quite often in her district, whilst Arthur Harding thought that women drinking was a 'terrible business', a 'terrifying thing' because they did not sip but drank like 'bloody navvies'. Birmingham's Medical Officer of Health reported in 1900 that most of the gross cases of neglect of the home and children were associated with drunkenness on the part of one or both of the parents, although he could not determine how far this drunkenness was induced in the first place by the miserable surroundings of slum life. Oral evidence tends to support this assertion but also reveals, in contrast to the opinions of many middle-class contemporaries, that moderate drinking did not necessarily lead to a deterioration in the cleanliness of a woman, her home or her children.

A lack of cleanliness was a fault attributed not only to drunkenness but also to the fact of a woman working. It was felt that the short time left to her after her employment made it more difficult for her to accomplish her household tasks, and this only exacerbated the naturally slovenly character of most women of the urban poor. It cannot be denied that there were many families who wallowed in filth and, given the maternal dominance of most lower-working-class families, that this lack of cleanliness could be blamed on a mother who was remiss in her duties. In their account of the home life and social environment of children in an industrial slum district in the 1940s, Arthur Collis and Vera G. Poole described the condition of one home they visited. The scene, as oral evidence confirms, would not have been unfamiliar in the period 1900–39. In the kitchen was a washing stand against the wall, on top of which was a basin of dirty water in which the children had been washed. Beside the basin was the milk and on the shelf below, beside the chamber pot, the butter. An enormous pile of dirty clothes filled one corner and in another was the coal. Over the floor was a litter of children's playthings and rubbish. At the table, covered with dirty china, uncooked vegetables and a pile of banana skins, sat a prostitute. The eldest girl of the family stood by the fireplace, cleaning the family comb with a pin, with which she then cleaned between her teeth. All the while the mother, who was only partly dressed, was roaring and swearing at two other girls that she would have them put away.

It was in order to counter what were seen as the dirty habits of the poor that councils began to employ women health visitors. The specific brief to each group of visitors engaged by a council differed only in slight respects from town to town and city to city. In general, the aim was to visit every house in a given district – nearly always a poor neighbourhood; to repeat that visit if it was thought necessary, and also to call on all homes where a mother had given birth. Health visitors were instructed to inquire into the deaths of all infants under one and to report any cases they thought should be brought before the attention of the Society for the Prevention of Cruelty to Children. In their role as 'teachers' seeking to improve those practices of the lower working class which were seen as unhealthy and which resulted in harmful living conditions, they gave out leaflets regarding the care and feeding of infants; they informed women as to how they should clean the house, wash clothes, destroy refuse and ventilate rooms; they were allowed to sell or give away carbolic soap so that rooms might be cleaned, and they could give away lime and lead brushes so that families might limewash the rooms, yards and outbuildings of their houses and, finally, they were able to hand out disinfecting powder so long as they explained its use. Some recognition was made of the fact that health visitors should be seen not just as instructors whose sole purpose was to admonish the poor, but also as advisers and, more importantly, helpers. The Birmingham Women's Settlement also acted on this principle, believing that its workers should endeavour to act truly as neighbours in a forlorn neighbourhood. In this capacity of acting as neighbours, health visitors were asked to help nurse the sick and to recommend hospitalisation if necessary; they were empowered to lend out maternity bags, sheets, pillow-cases and nightdresses to the sick, and, in an important move designed to assure the poor that they were concerned with the effects of environment as much as with their characters, they had to report all nuisances and sanitary defects to the local Inspector of Nuisances.

Birmingham appointed four women health visitors in 1898, following the lead given by Manchester, Liverpool, Glasgow and Chesterfield. Dr Hill reported in the following year that the work these women had done had been a striking success, resulting in a very marked and permanent improvement in the homes of the poor. Over the next few years Birmingham began, as did other towns and cities, to engage more health visitors, some of whose original tasks became the responsibility of more specialist women workers employed by councils. By 1910 the city was divided into fifteen districts, each with its own health visitor who was responsible to a superintendent. Two years later the number of districts was increased to nineteen – the duties of whose visitors were expanded to include making a special inspection of schoolchildren who had been accepted by the Country Holiday Schemes (some charities paid for holidays in the country for the young of the poor). The task of the women in this respect was to ensure that the children were tidy, clean and free from infections. It was also felt necessary to employ an

assistant superintendent, four infant visitors, one inspector of
midwives, nine tuberculosis visitors and two inspectors of
workshops. All of these were women. 1919 saw the number of
health visitors, for the first time distinguished by the prefix of
general, rise to seventy-eight, whilst their responsibilities now
included giving talks and health lectures to mothers' meetings,
factory girls and others, as well as giving evidence at Police
Courts (the equivalent of Magistrates' Courts).

There is no doubt that the services of officials such as those
described were needed, and it is obvious that they were essential
in educating those of the poor who did not keep themselves or
their homes clean. In 1899, 11,700 houses were visited in
Birmingham, of which 3,000 were regarded as needing to be
revisited because of the dirty condition of the homes. Some 894
houses were regarded as badly in need of cleaning; in some cases
the filthiness was regarded as indescribable and the visitors
kept calling on these homes until cleanliness was achieved. A
total of 933 families were required to empty bedroom slops,
whilst in 212 homes the bedding needed cleaning. In some homes
this was described as horribly filthy and so full of vermin that
large numbers of mattresses had to be burned. The work of the
women health visitors in Birmingham was aided by voluntary
agencies. There existed a sanitary council and some parishes
organised scrubbing services; on a certain day the vicar would
call on all parishioners to come and scrub the church clean, an
action which was preceded by a short religious service. This
practice was supposed to encourage the poor in the habit of
cleanliness. However, it became increasingly obvious to official
and voluntary workers that the environment of the districts in
which the poor dwelt was at least as important a reason for dirt
and unhealthy conditions as were the habits of some of the
inhabitants.

It is true that in the first year in which the system of health
visitors was introduced in Birmingham, 1,800 notices were
served on landlords requiring them to execute some sanitary
work on their properties. Furthermore, a recognition was made
of the fact that the 'inadequacy and publicity of the closet
accommodation' was indeed one of the glaring faults connected
with the back-to-back homes of the city. Yet Dr Hill remained
staunch in his belief that the unhealthiness of the lower-class

districts, as he described them, was largely the result of the characteristics of the people who lived in them. It was not until 1904, when he was replaced by Dr Robertson, that amongst city officials the balance began to tilt towards the view that, whilst personal traits were important, it was environment which was the dominant factor in affecting cleanliness in poor neighbourhoods. In his report of 1913, the doctor expressly stated that due regard ought to be paid to the fact that a large majority of sanitary conveniences in slum areas were shared by two or more families, and that these were continually broken open and occasionally slept in by vagrants. Furthermore, numbers of houses contained no water supply and all water for personal ablutions had to be heated over the kitchen fire. By 1918 he was of the strong belief that the majority of slum-dwellers would be decent and clean if they were given the chance. Importantly, he also recognised that, whilst there existed a small proportion of the poor who were thriftless and criminal, this was the case in all ranks in society. The only fact which distinguished those who belonged to the poor was that they were more noticeable than the thriftless among the higher classes. Finally, in 1924, Dr Robertson emphasised that, to a very large extent, environment could be changed and with its improvement could come an uplifting in the habits of the poor.

The kind of living conditions which confronted and challenged the inhabitants of slum districts were expressively set out in 1901 in a series of articles by J. Cuming Walters in *The Birmingham Daily Gazette*:

Look at the houses, the alleys, the courts, the ill-lit, ill-paved walled in squares, with last night's rain still trickling down from the rooves and making pools of the ill-sluiced yards. Look at the begrimed windows, the broken glass, the apertures stopped with yellow paper or filthy rags, glance at the rooms where large families eat and sleep every day and every night amongst rags and vermin within dank and mildewed walls from which the blistered paper is drooping or the bit of discolouration called 'paint' is peeling away. Here you can veritably taste the pestilential air, stagnant and nephitic, which finds no outlet in the prison like houses of the courts; and yet here where there is a breathing space for so few, the many are herded together and overcrowding is the rule not the exception . . . The poor have nowhere else to go. It is here amid the rank and rotting garbage, in the filthy alleys and the time-blackened, old fashioned dwellings, near the ill-smelling canal; or in the vicinage of factories which pour out their fumes in billowing masses from the throats of giant stacks – here it is they must come to shelter.[26]

During the 1920s and 1930s Birmingham, in common with many other industrial towns and cities, embarked on a programme of slum clearance coupled with the building of vast numbers of municipal houses in which the displaced poor could be accommodated in a very much healthier environment. Yet, despite the urgency of the programme, hundreds of thousands of people throughout England's industrial areas continued to live in inadequate, insanitary and unhealthy homes which crowded the older, central districts of a town. As late as 1960 there still lingered 25,000 back-to-back houses in Birmingham alone.

In the face of horrendous living conditions and an environment as hostile to cleanliness as that described by Cuming Walters, it is little surprise that many families succumbed and ceased to battle against their surroundings. The wonder is that so many did not. Large numbers of families, inspired by the diligence of their women, continued the struggle to remain clean in home and self. Furthermore, in most cases this type of family was not stimulated by the activities of health visitors or voluntary workers; the real success of these was in affecting the habits of the marginally dirty and untidy. Cleanliness was not a virtue taught to the lower working class by the middle class. Hundreds of thousands of poor families had been clean before the advent of workers employed by a council to induce cleanliness amongst them, as indicated by Andrew Mearns in 1883 when, in *The Bitter Cry of Outcast London*, he described how a mother who was dying of dropsy kept her children the cleanest and tidiest in the Board School. This kind of woman kept herself and her family clean not because she had to, not because authority forced her to, but because she herself wished it to be so. The poor did not wallow in dirt; the wives and daughters – it was beneath a man's dignity to clean – toiled endlessly to ensure this. In *Canary Girls and Stockpots*, set in Luton around the time of the First World War, Edith Hall declared that the greatest stigma against a woman was to be considered lazy. This was as true for lower-working-class wives as it was for those of the upper working class, perhaps even more so, because the environment of the more affluent was not as unfriendly to cleanliness as was that of the poor. For these, laziness in a woman was inevitably followed by a dirty home and unkempt children.

To remain clean required hard work. In Salford, Roberts reported that the great Friday-night scouring ritual included the participation of all the women of a house. Indeed, local dance halls closed on that evening because there was a lack of girls to attend them. Throughout the nation the routine included similar tasks: scrubbing downstairs floors tiled with red quarries (a brick-like form of unglazed tiles); scrubbing the family's table white, as well as the stairs and floor boards upstairs; black-leading the grate and polishing the ornaments that hung around it; 'whitening' the hearth, and finally red ochring the front step, or in Manchester, as described by Walter Greenwood, using brown or white stone. This last task was the means whereby the outward signs of a wife's cleanliness were proudly proclaimed to all and sundry. As John Douglas discerningly observed, dirt could be ankle-deep on the floor, cardboard might be patching up broken window panes, banana boxes could be the one form of seating, coats the only form of blanket and a jam jar the only kind of chamber pot, yet if a family's front step was not scrubbed once a week, and if the grate was not black-leaded, then the wife was dirty and not worth anything. It was also important for the status of a family that toilets be kept scrupulously clean. Kathleen Dayuss recalled that, in the yard she lived in as a child, there were five outside toilets for ten families, and that there were constant rows as to which wife's turn it was to clean them. Finally, her father put a big padlock on one of them and gave his wife and the woman next-door a key, and the two of them ensured that this particular water closet was kept clean. This was a further indication of the prestige of Dayuss's mother because the other closets were left open for anyone to use and became filthy.

Rats posed a problem in some of the very poorest districts. The Reverend T. J. Bass recounted how one family in his parish guarded over their young daughter's body to protect it from the marauding rodents. However, one form of vermin was impossible to eradicate from a home, no matter how clean, and thus the presence of these in a house did not lower the standing of a family. House bugs thrived in the damp, crumbling mortar which held together jerry-built slum dwellings. They smelled vile and occupiers tried many means to be rid of them: a stick of sulphur would be broken on an enamel plate and then ignited in the hope of the fumes driving the bugs out; candles would be used to burn them off the walls and ceiling, or even paraffin would be run around the bed to provide it with a protective perimeter. In the end, all proved ineffectual, as did the occasional fumigation of a house. Vermin of the head and body were also widespread. A report from Birmingham in 1913 showed that thirty per cent of the children who were inspected at the city's schools were infected with lice in the head or body, or both. The prevalence of these vermin was aided by the habit of buying second-hand clothes, the lack of a change of clothes, and inadequacy of combs and an insufficiency of washing utensils. Both types were regarded with distaste by the poor – especially bodily vermin – and, despite the difficulty of avoiding them, their presence or otherwise were seen as indicative of a family's cleanliness in the eyes of the rest of the community. Kathleen Dayuss remembered that her mother forbade her to play with children who had 'dirty heads', although she still did. On one occasion she was found to be infected and her father poured paraffin over her head and then cut all her hair off. A ritual once a week in most households was the combing of a child's hair with a fine-tooth comb to make sure its head was clean. Cleanliness in children was an important indicator of a family's position in lower-working-class society. The mother of a woman from Paddington called her children to her bedside following each confinement. She would then proceed to wash every one, intent on ensuring that her condition did not allow the family's standards of cleanliness to drop. A Birmingham woman shared the same memory. Her mother's other actions also gave the lie to Patterson's opinion that the children of the poor never learned to blow their noses and grew content to breathe through their mouths, sniffling all their days. This mother, like many others, pinned a piece of clean rag onto her daughters' dresses each day before they went to school, so that this might act as a handkerchief.

Of course, cleanliness in the home and in children was not more important than cleanliness in a woman. To receive the compliment of 'spotless' in all three was an accolade worthy of the hard work necessary to attain it. In Birmingham a regular practice amongst wives was to lock their front doors once they had seen their younger children off to school and their husbands and older children off to work. During the course of the day this would be the only time that doors would be locked. Once safely enclosed in her home, a woman would strip down from top to bottom and wash herself thoroughly. After this she would put on a clean 'frock' and 'pinny' and then might curl her hair with one of the fire irons. Staying clean was difficult; it was very easy to slip into a state of 'half-cleanliness' and even slovenliness as Helen Forrester's middle-class mother found. Within a few weeks of arriving in the slums her dress hung loosely on her; shining, black hair – which had been exquisitely kept by her hairdresser – had grown long and straggling; her face had become haggard and lined, and the polished ovals of her nails were ruined by her having to bite them so as to shorten them. Moreover, her baby's back had become sore where the urine had not been properly washed off, whilst the infant's head was full of scurf. Faced by the problems of slum life, Forrester's mother almost gave way, at one stage breaking down and screaming that she could take no more.

In the issue of cleanliness the importance of matriarchs, the keepers of the common consciousness of the poor and custodians of their standards of behaviour, can again be perceived. The cleanliness of a family and its home was to be worn like a badge of honour; its dirtiness as a symbol of its shame and particularly that of its wife. As a Birmingham woman commented of the 1920s and 1930s, a wife who was not clean would be hounded, especially if there was a row between two women. When this occurred, the distaste of the community in general would be publicly aired by the protagonist who was the cleaner. Dr Robertson tended to the view that bad habits were catching, that those families who would normally have led clean and healthy lives were contaminated by dirty neighbours. Of course, this could and did happen. However, it is notable that the discriminating observer of the poor could detect a division of lower-working-class neighbourhoods into two kinds: those where the inhabitants, as Cuming Walters saw it, were despairing, and lived as if a blight rested on all, and those where the people were just as deep in poverty but were distinguished by a cheerful, persevering and aspiring temperament. This 'schism' of the poor can be partly attributed to the 'hounding' of the dirty who, as a result, clustered together in certain districts. Collis and Poole provided an example of how this could occur. From 1929 the Goodmans had been regarded as a 'problem' family by official and voluntary services. On one occasion they were rehoused in a new block of flats. Slum clearance meant that subtle differences of status within the lower working class were ignored or unnoticed by officials so that, as in this instance, a 'dirty' family could be set down in the midst of those who were clean. Consequently, it was not long before the neighbours of the Goodmans began to complain about the family. They were upset by the disgusting condition of their flat, by the appearance of the children, and also by Mrs Goodman's bad language. It seems likely that if the family had lived in an established community in the years before the Second World War, then the open disgust of their neighbours might have forced them to seek alternative accommodation.

The separation of 'dirty' and 'clean' families in the years 1880–1939 should not be regarded as anywhere near total, nor is it suggested that there was a rigid demarcation between the two. Families who were clean could often be forced by circumstances to live in a 'dirty' district; the husband's job might be nearby, or the houses could be cheaper. It was these who were most susceptible to the 'catching of bad habits' which Dr Robertson mentioned. Conversely, dirty families lived in 'clean' neighbourhoods and it would appear, except in the case of the incorrigible like the Goodmans, that the effect of the general opinion of their neighbours was at least as great a factor in encouraging them to raise their standards as was the activity of official workers, and Ellen Ross has noticed this in respect of London. A further and socially serious complaint against the Goodmans was that the wife was accused of immorality. Amongst the poor the connection between 'loose living' and dirtiness in a person was often made. It is certainly true that prostitutes found it easier to carry on their activities in a district which was considered as 'dirty' or 'rough' according to the perceptions of the lower working class. Moreover, these areas were also those in which the nature of family life was less stable and the community less 'settled'. It is important to be aware of this. Mrs Goodman, like many mothers of problem families, was separated from her husband. This, and the practice of living together, was common in unsettled districts and, as many sociological studies have shown, in this kind of area where 'broken' families and prostitutes flourished side by side, respect for women was lowered. In contrast, this increased in those neighbourhoods which were settled and it is in these, where women were generally respected and where family life was essential to the growth of community, that the hidden matriarchy flourished. Where the poor prized cleanliness, praised hard work and admired strength, then it took a woman who was characterised by all three and who also possessed a skill which was valued to become transformed into a matriarch.

This discussion in itself would seem to provide enough evidence to suggest that it was incorrect to equate a dirty home with a working wife. In general, women who sought employment were not the infirm, the chronically ill or the incapacitated, most of whom could not work anyway, nor were they the feckless, or the hopeless who drifted along with the tide of poverty and did not swim against it. Instead, they were women who were united by a desire to improve the living conditions of their families and to maintain a certain status. It is difficult to quantify their cleanliness or otherwise. The Birmingham report of 1906 did state that, of the homes of the 771 industrially employed mothers which were visited, 400 were satisfactory in their cleanliness and 371 were neglected to a greater or lesser degree. It would be interesting to know exactly what this latter phrase meant, but more revealing would have been a comparison with a similar number of homes of mothers who were not industrially employed. However, the comments of Dr Duncan, who was an authority on the living conditions of the poor through her experience and work in the slums of Birmingham, are very meaningful. In her opinion, the married working woman was more vigorous and determined in her efforts to stave off poverty than was the wife who remained at home. Clementina Black concurred with this statement, expressing the belief that it was the homes and children of the wives of her Class A which were most conspicuously neglected. Naturally, due allowance needs to be made for the sections of the poor who today would be cared for by the social services, an

allowance which Black made. For these, work and attempts at
cleanliness proved daunting tasks. Yet nothing should detract
from the problems which faced wives who worked and who also
kept the home. A life of unremitting toil can only emphasise
their dedication to their families and their emotional and
physical strength.

Chapter four

Survival

This book has been concerned with dispelling the notion that the women of the urban poor were so dispirited by poverty's inexorable advance that they accepted defeat and became its passive victims. The evidence to the contrary is abundant and emphasises that many women were active; they fought back against privation and, within their communities, against the society which allowed it to spread so wantonly. Armoured by the devotion of their children, supplying themselves and their families with the resources provided by their wages, their bodies and their spirits, women were not only the foot soldiers of the poor in the battle against want, they were also the generals. The success of many women in the war of attrition waged by poverty was not won without cost. As with any conflict, those in the forefront suffered the heaviest casualties and the triumph of many families was marred by the loss of its mother through death or her incapacity as a result of illness.

Margery Spring Rice listed the ailments which had the greatest incidence amongst the wives who contributed to her survey. The list included anaemia; headaches – for which only thirty per cent of the women were professionally treated; constipation, with or without haemorrhoids; rheumatism – which was regarded, along with the previous three complaints, as inevitable; gynaecological trouble; carious teeth and toothache, and varicose veins, ulcerated legs, white leg and phlebitis. Of the wives included, sixty per cent had bad legs of one kind or another. This was not an exhaustive list, as backache, respiratory trouble, kidney disorders, weariness and depression, and many other ailments were common in the women as a result of poverty, courageous neglect, self-abnegation and their pre-judice and fear of seeking medical advice. Surprisingly, omitted from the causes of exhaustion and ill-health was one particu-larly relevant to the poor, that of a high birth-rate. In 1900 the life expectancy of a woman aged twenty was forty-six years. She could expect to spend a third of that time pregnant or nursing infants, with the consequent effect on her of ill-health and premature ageing.

The second half of the decade 1870–80 saw the birth-rate of England and Wales entering a progressive annual decline. If the number of women of childbearing age – fifteen to forty-five – was calculated, then the proportion of total births per 1,000 women of that group was 153·7 in 1870–2, 147·7 in 1880–2, 129·7 in 1890–2 and 114·8 in 1900–2. These figures represented a tremendous fall which was at first thought to be the result of a connection with the trade cycle and its effect on the marriage rate. By the turn of the century, it was revealed that this was not so. The declining birth-rate had no connection with the marriage rate, a slight connection with the increasing numbers of people who were marrying later, but was mainly due to causes over which the individual had control. In the euphemisms of the era, this meant couples using means of birth control to limit the size of their families. The Report of the Registrar General in 1905 emphasised this: he attributed seventeen per cent of the fall to the later age of marriage of couples; ten per cent to the decrease in illegitimacy, and seventy-three per cent to a deliberate restriction on child-bearing by married people.

This decline in the birth-rate was not, however uniform. In 1907 Dr Robertson noticed that the birth-rate in Birmingham corresponded closely with the class of people who lived in the various areas of the city, and that if it had been possible to make a birth-rate which was related to class, then it would have been found that in the middle and upper classes the rate was very low. Thus, in 1900 the city's most salubrious, middle-class ward, Edgbaston and Harborne, recorded a birth-rate of 18·6 per 1,000 of the population, whilst the generally upper-working-class ward of Balsall Heath registered a rate of 24·3. In comparison, the birth-rate in the poor, central ward of St Stephen's was 36·9 and that of the equally lower-working-class Duddeston ward 37·3, a rate for the latter exactly the same as was recorded in the

Rhondda. Mining districts have been regarded as distinguished by a high birth-rate in this period for two reasons: firstly, because the earning capacity of men in these areas was maximised early and so they tended to marry at an earlier age than elsewhere, and secondly, because in districts dominated by one industry employing only men, the job prospects open to women were limited. It is interesting that in Birmingham's poor areas, where so many married women worked, the birth-rate compared with those of mining areas.

The discrepancy between the birth-rates of the various wards of Birmingham remained marked through the 1920s and 1930s, although distinguished from the mid-1920s by a fall in that registered in poor wards as well as in those for better-off wards. In 1924 the average decrease in the lower-working-class central wards was 7·3 per 1,000 on the average birth-rate for 1912–14; that for the middle-ring wards (mostly upper working class) 7·9, and for the suburban outer wards 7·0. By 1930 the birth-rate for the central wards had fallen to 21·3, but slum clearance and the rehousing of the poor meant that some outer wards had a much higher rate than the average for these areas of 16·2. For example, Perry Barr, where there were large numbers of council houses, recorded a rate of 27·7. The trend was clear, however, not only in Birmingham but in other industrial towns and cities. Decades after the middle class and then the upper working class had begun to limit the size of their families, the poor too were deciding to reduce the number of their children. That many women of the urban poor had always wanted to do so is beyond question. No matter how devoted a mother, the prospect of perhaps twenty-five years of child-bearing could not have been eagerly anticipated. As Acorn, a man, sighed of his younger siblings who seemed to continually increase in number, 'Oh, those everlasting babies; as soon as one could toddle, another needed nursing.'

Children required care and care included time, which always seemed restricted to a mother of the poor. Furthermore, the proper care of infants was rendered more difficult in slum areas than in suburban districts by the dangers inherent in living in poverty. Infant mortality rates for lower-working-class areas were always higher: for example, in 1905 the figure registered for Edgbaston and Harborne was 131 per 1,000 live births, compared with 207 in the very poor Birmingham ward of St Bartholomew's. Additionally, whilst the general death rate for the city was falling, its infant mortality rate remained stable; the figure of 195 deaths per 1,000 live births in 1904 was virtually the same as that for 1875. The main reason for this was the enormous mortality of infants in lower-working-class districts which was caused by diarrhoea and whooping cough. Both diseases thrived in insanitary conditions. Some mothers exacerbated their babies' chances of dying by feeding them out of dirty bottles – if they were hand-fed; by using the old type of india-rubber tube bottle which was especially harmful to infants, and by feeding their very young in the same manner as they would adults when they were on solids. To counter these problems, in the early twentieth century, at the same time as councils improved or cleared slum property and improved sanitation, a programme of educating mothers of the poor in the best way of raising and feeding their infants was embarked on. Handbills were distributed and posters put up giving information on how to take precautions against consumption, typhoid fever, diarrhoea, measles and whooping cough, and health visitors were employed. Dr Robertson observed perceptively in 1916 that nature did not endow any mother with the necessary information on how to shield her infant from the dangers which surrounded it in a civilised community; amongst the rich, as well as the poor, there was evidence of a need for instruction.

A further cause of the high infant mortality rates in poor districts was recognised in the unhealthy condition of many pregnant women. This also affected the health of children who survived. Healthy children were dependent on a healthy mother who lived in healthy surroundings and who was able to preserve her health in pregnancy. To help facilitate these objectives in Birmingham, three small voluntary societies from 1914 provided substantial and suitable dinners at a nominal cost of a penny for mothers, expectant and nursing, who were found by health visitors and other lady visitors to be insufficiently fed during the winter months. Some of the middle class felt that this practice was harmful as it took away from the husband the responsibility of providing for his wife. Their argument was confounded by the fact that most of the women helped had sick husbands and were struggling to bring up large families – the average number of babies per mother at one centre was five – without recourse to Parish Relief. Another feature found worthy of praise in these women was that they stopped attending when they were able to provide for themselves and paid up any arrears that they owed. A total of 8,465 meals were provided during the winter of 1914–15. By 1918 the city council had established five Maternity Feeding Centres charging twopence per dinner. High unemployment in 1922 resulted in the addition of two more centres and in that year nearly 30,000 meals were provided, 11,000 up on the previous year.

The post-war period saw the establishment of other facilities to help the nursing and expectant mother, in Birmingham as elsewhere. In 1920 a maternity home was opened at Heathfield Road with 185 beds, followed in 1921 by another at Penns Lane with seventy-nine beds. A convalescent home for mothers and babies was established at Pype Hayes Hall with 380 beds. Local welfare centres were opened, with facilities for X-rays, dental treatment, infant welfare – including an observation ward – and for education in breast-feeding to be found at Carnegie Infant Welfare Centre. A babies' hospital was opened at Witton in 1921 and from 1920 home helps were employed to cook and clean during the confinement of a mother, although these were busiest in upper-working-class areas. Increasingly in the 1920s too, mothers were sent to Dudley Road or Selly Oak Hospitals for their confinements if the condition of their homes was considered inadequate. Without doubt, the programme of slum clearance and providing the poor with houses in a healthier environment, allied to a campaign of educating mothers in health care as well as providing them with the support of a burgeoning welfare service, paid dividends nationally. In Birmingham, success was gauged by the fact that infant mortality dropped to sixty per thousand live births – the lowest ever – in 1930, and although that in the central wards with a figure of eighty was still higher than the outer wards with a figure of forty-nine, there is no denying that the poor had benefited enormously by council action.

Yet, although undoubted improvements in the health of the poor were achieved, the statement made by F. B. Smith in his article 'Health' in *The Working Class in England 1875–1914*, edited by John Benson, would appear pertinent to their condition. He believed that, despite decades of social engineering and expensive medical intervention, people in the poorest class still experienced higher morbidity and mortality rates than did people in other classes. This is difficult to quantify with regard to women of the urban poor specifically, but it would appear likely that whilst their life-expectancy was rising in line with that of women in general, and was greatly helped by a declining birth-rate, it still lagged behind that of more prosperous women. It would also seem that their general health remained worse, as the evidence in an earlier chapter regarding malnutrition in women in the 1930s and 1940s would indicate. In support of this assertion, the Newcastle investigation quoted by John Burnett showed that twenty-one per cent of the women included in the sample were anaemic, but of the wives of the unemployed, thirty-three per cent were anaemic. Slum clearance, too, was not always beneficial to a woman's health, as was made clear by the experiments of Lady Williams in the Rhondda in 1934. New houses cost more in rent and, because they were usually on the outskirts of built-up areas, the members of a family had to spend more money on reaching work. As a result, less money could be spent on food and this had a particularly disastrous effect on expectant mothers. Lady Williams observed that no improvement in ante-natal care reduced the high rates of maternal mortality until food was distributed to them. When this was done the rate fell by a massive seventy five per cent. The health of the women of the urban poor was improving, but at a much slower pace than was greatly needed to improve their quality of life.

Throughout the period 1880–1939 many women of the urban poor must have wished to limit their families purely because of the toll death took of their young, especially in larger families, although it is interesting to note that Kathleen Dayuss thought that the poor continued having children to make up for those who died. There remained, however, an even more compelling reason for a wife to wish for a small family and that was the serious effect which the bearing of large numbers of children had on their own health. As one woman in Margaret Llewellyn Davies's book on maternity stated with dismay, she was a ruined woman through having children. Sherard, too, was of the opinion that children were an impediment to a woman of the urban poor and that motherhood was a curse to her. A number of circumstances adversely affected a woman's health. Firstly, she ate little and what she did eat was not nutritious and did not strengthen her when this was essential. Secondly, women continued to work at their employment for as long before their confinements as possible. 205 of the mothers in the 1908 Birmingham survey remained at their jobs to within three months of the expected date of their delivery, whilst a further 140, or twenty-three per cent of the total, worked up to within one week of their confinement. Everyday household tasks also had to be carried on, many of them strenuous in their nature: washing, cleaning, scrubbing, polishing, carrying coal and water and looking after other children; all had to be continued, as Lady Bell said, right up to the very last minute before a birth. Sherard quoted the case of one mother who worked at making chains – a very heavy and hard job – until two and a quarter hours before she gave birth, immediately before which she cleaned the house. Thirdly, although the law forbade an employer from knowingly engaged a mother within four weeks of her pregnancy, many mothers returned to work within that period. In the Birmingham sample fifty-seven did so. What the law did not forbid, as Clementina Black pointed out, was a mother performing arduous tasks in the house which could also prove harmful to her health. Fourthly, there came problems related to the birth itself, at which most women of the poor did not have chloroform to help mitigate the pain.

Many births in a lower-working-class neighbourhood were not attended by a midwife or doctor, or else were supervised by a local midwife who was often old, ignorant, dirty and illiterate. The Midwives Act of 1902 sought to root out these practitioners of midwifery. In 1905 the first section of this Act came into operation. It decreed that there should be certified midwives and uncertified. These latter were not entitled to call themselves midwives, but were allowed to practise as such and to take fees until April 1910 when they had to cease their trade if they remained uncertified. Between April and 31 December 1905, 221 women registered themselves under the Act in Birmingham. The dangers presented to the mothers of the poor by many midwives were made startlingly clear when it was revealed that fifty-two of the women could not read or write and had never received any instruction as to how to conduct a confinement. Others had as their only guide a cheap translation of one of the works of Hippocrates. Over the next few years matters did improve: there were classes to teach the women about confinement; they were required to be clean and to possess a bag with the apparatus in it; there was a course on the feeding and raising of children, and finally an examination. However, dirty and incapable midwives remained. In 1905 it was reported that two had been drunk at confinements, and in the case of one birth the midwife had sent for medical help too late, with the result that the patient was damaged for life, whilst in another a mother died for the same reason. In 1906 comment was made as to the dirtiness of the hands and nails of many midwives who practised in the slums, and another instance in tardiness in calling for medical help resulted in the baby becoming blind through developing serious ophthalmia. The implementation of the second part of the Midwives Act in 1910, which disallowed non-certified midwives from practising, finally brought about the required change in the nature of these women. There did remain a compelling reason, however, why mothers of the poor did not have a midwife at their birth – other than through a lack of confidence in their abilities – and that was the cost. In 1908 the average fee was 8s 6d, around half a week's wages for a labourer in work, rising to an average of fifteen shillings in 1916, or 12s 6d if the husband alone was insured under the National Insurance Act of 1911. One final problem confronted a woman of the lower working class when she gave birth. If a midwife thought medical assistance was necessary, it proved very difficult to obtain the services of a doctor if the mother lived in a poor neighbourhood. Doctors were reluctant to attend because of the inability of the poor to pay them, although some feared a loss of reputation if a patient died, even if they could not have helped. To counteract this tendency in Birmingham, the Board of Guardians of the parish were prepared to pay for the services of the nearest medical man called in by a midwife, whom the city's Health Committee supplied with cards for use on these occasions. Non-attendance of doctors remained a problem until 1917 when the Public Health Committee took over responsibility for their payment.

Deaths in childbirth were not uncommon; in 1903 Dr Robertson reported that in Birmingham one mother died in every 264 births from puerperal fever (infection of the uterus), from accidents, or from parturition (the act of childbirth). Death in this latter case was particularly horrifying. In 1880 the death of Eliza Finney was investigated at Birmingham Coroner's Court. It was revealed that, immediately after the birth, blood poured so greatly from this woman living in a poor neighbourhood that it soaked through the mattress onto the floor. A doctor's assistant arrived and gave brandy and extract of beef to staunch the flow of blood and then removed the afterbirth. His actions proved ineffectual; the blood kept flooding out of the unfortunate woman until it caused her death. A fear of childbirth, as well as a desire to limit their families and not increase the burden of their responsibilities, might have appeared to predispose the poor to a use of contraception. This was not the case. As Roberts stated, birth control, at least till the early 1920s, was regarded as a sin against the Holy Ghost. Husbands were often particularly vehemently opposed to its use. Madeline Kerr noticed this attitude lingering on in the 1950s in Ship Street. She attributed its cause to the fact that, in a community where the woman was dominant, the male tended to cling to the last vestige of his power by refusing to allow his wife to be sterilised or to use methods of birth control. My own oral evidence supports this statement, suggesting that many men regarded a large family as a public display of their manhood. There is little doubt that this attitude, conjoined with a belief that contraception was morally wrong, was important in militating against the widespread use of methods of birth control amongst the poor. Nevertheless, it would seem that the major reason for their lack of use was neither of these; instead, it could be attributed to the general ignorance, verging at times on innocence, of the poor regarding sexual matters.

With an insider's awareness, Roberts claimed that, though the Edwardian masses were earthy, this was only so in strictly limited social situations. He believed that respectability ran deep through working-class womanhood; that this was how their men wanted it, and that the lower working class as a whole remained philistine and sexually inhibited. Indeed, he could not envisage that women of the urban poor were any subject at all for orgiastic pleasure, nor were their men much freer. Sex was not regarded as an act in which women were expected to receive satisfaction. As Dolly Scannel stated, it was a man's prerogative to ask but a woman must never, never ask, although it was her duty not to refuse her husband. It is with regard to sexual relations between husbands and wives that Leonore Davidoff's assertion as to the subservience of women to men in marriage is at its most apposite. For not even the strongest and most assertive matriarch would believe it correct to acknowledge, at least publicly, that she refused her husband his marital rights. Indeed, the oral evidence suggests very strongly that, especially before 1914, many men would beat their unwilling wives into agreeing to satisfy their urges. The acquiescence of strong women, as well as others, in the belief that they should submit to their husbands on the occasions they demanded sex can only be judged in the context of the era in which they lived. Sex for enjoyment was looked on as a function which was peculiar to men; it was not in the sphere of matters in which women were involved, and so even very independent wives would have found it strange to withhold their consent, even though they found little pleasure in the act themselves. The attitude of many women towards sex must have resembled that adopted by Mrs Turpin towards her husband when he was drunk; it was an incident in the possession of a husband which was as inevitable as acquiring children, but its occurrence was to be kept as infrequent as was possible.

It must be noted, however, that the oral evidence also indicates that some women did find pleasure in sex, and this is especially apparent from the 1920s onwards if they were married to sympathetic husbands. Obviously, this kind of evidence is difficult to quantify, and it is made more difficult to assess because many wives associated their own sexual satisfaction with harlotry, and thus were ashamed to admit to it. There are also intriguing hints in the oral evidence suggesting that women who enjoyed sex were present before 1914. This evidence is inevitably associated with married women who went off with men other than their husbands, and it is as invariably linked to the phrase that they were 'over-sexed'. It would be wrong to take the implications of this evidence too far, but I feel that it does indicate that wives in the period 1880–1939 were perhaps not all indifferent to sex, and that the stifling oppression of respectability has prevented this from emerging more fully. Moreover, in many cases those women who may have found gratification from sex when they were first married must have lost any desire they had, once the realisation dawned that sexual pleasure for a woman had to be paid for in the pain of childbirth. For the majority of the women of the urban poor, true sexual fulfilment was impossible in the absence of effective contraception.

Sex was not a matter for public, nor very often intimate, discussion, and sex education for the children of the urban poor remained totally inadequate throughout the 1920s and 1930s. Any matter concerned with a woman's body was taboo. Few girls knew about periods until the day they appeared. On discovering her first period, Kathleen Dayuss believed that she was going to bleed to death and, on informing her mother, she was told simply that from then on she was to stay away from the lads and not kiss them or else she would end up pregnant. As late as 1947 one Birmingham woman remembered that she was carried home from school at the age of eleven, suffering from her first period. Her mother's only reaction was to throw a sanitary towel on the bed where she lay without explaining its use. Indeed, although the disposable sanitary towel had been patented as far back as 1892, it is unlikely that many lower-working-class women used them before the Second World War. Instead, pieces of clean rag, often made from bed linen, were used, washed and continually reused.

Old wives' tales forbade the washing of a woman's hair or feet whilst she had a period, because it was felt that she would go 'barmy' if she did. The feeling persisted that at the time of menstruation a woman was unclean and, in an interesting affirmation of this sentiment up to the 1920s, in poor parts of Birmingham some women wore a piece of red rag around their wrist when out in public to indicate to all and sundry that they were menstruating. In connection with this matter of the unclean nature of women at certain times in their lives, mention must be made of churching. This aspect of 'festive Christianity' – that is, the observance by the nominally Christian of religious rituals such as christenings, marriages and funerals – was especially vigorous amongst the urban poor, as Hugh McLeod has noticed. It also seems peculiarly High Church in its observance (although I have oral evidence which indicates that it was also popular amongst urban Roman Catholics). Church-ing itself was an act of ritual cleansing, and also thanksgiving, whereby a mother of a new baby was accepted back into the community. Many of my women interviewees from Birmingham have stated how they were not allowed into the homes of anyone else, even those of relatives, until the local vicar had 'churched' them. Consequently, churching usually took place as soon as possible after a birth. The practice was still adhered to strongly in the 1950s, as indicated by this oral testimony and by Young and Willmott in their study.

The lack of communication apparent between mothers and daughters with regard to periods was even more marked in respect of sex. The naïvety of working-class women in sexual matters has been remarked upon by Elizabeth Roberts in connection with her oral evidence, and my own interviews substantiate her comment. As a Birmingham woman who reached her teens in the mid-1920s recalled:

'Cus our Mom never used to talk to us properly, she never used to say what was what. Now, what she used to say was, 'You bring so and so trouble here and you'll go 'op it'.
But she never told us what the trouble was, we never knew what the trouble was. All as we thought was stealing or anythink like that. We was always taught that if ever we touched anythink belonging to anyone else we'd 'ave our fingers chopped off. And if we told a lie we should 'ave our tongues cut out. And we used to believe that until we was old enough to realise it couldn't be done. But we never thought of any other trouble. Never tell you anythink about women's trouble. We neve used to know nothink. What we learned was off other kids and then it worn't in a proper manner. It was all wrong, but I suppose it was like that with everybody in them days.[27]

In settled, as opposed to unsettled neighbourhoods, where there were often fewer inhibitions sexually, moral respectability ensured the silence of mothers and their lack of information to their daughters about the functions of their bodies. Older children and, if a woman worked, wives in a factory were sources of instruction but the extent of this can be exaggerated, whilst it often took the unhelpful form of whispered and teasing hints. The case of a Birmingham woman who bore her first child at the age of twenty-four in 1936 emphasises this. She was the eldest daughter of a family of twelve and had helped her mother care for her younger brothers and sisters, and she had worked in a factory from the age of fourteen, yet months into her pregnancy she still did not know where the baby was to come from. When the mother of a friend told her the facts of birth she cried, ran home to her mother's and resolved not to go back to live with her husband. As she recalled, she was as innocent sexually as a new-born baby. Wyn Heywood verified this lack of knowledge. Sex was a dirty word in the vocabulary of her family; it was never discussed, always kept secret.

The concept of morality in most lower-working-class neighbourhoods was an important force of social control. Unmarried girls were scared to experiment sexually before they married because of the shame attached to illegitimacy. A regular admonition to a courting teenager was that it was a 'chap's place to ask, a girl's to say no'. Little matter that many young women did not know what they were supposed to say 'no' to. This moral code of the poor was not adhered to as a result of pressures imposed by a middle class intent on the poor adopting their moral values. In certain areas, and amongst a certain type of family, immorality was the norm, in spite of the efforts of the religious and others of the affluent. Where successful, the implementation of moral standards of behaviour was largely the result of the influence of the married women of a settled community. It was this, together with the practice of a courting couple marrying if a girl became pregnant, which was as great an influence in the decline of the national rate of illegitimacy as was the increased use of contraceptives. In 1870 this rate had stood at seventeen per 1,000 unmarried women aged fifteen to forty-five; by 1904 it had dropped to 8·4 and by 1920 to 3·6. The fall corresponds too closely to the establishment of settled communities amongst the poor and to the rise of a matriarchy within them to dismiss their significance. Interestingly, whilst great shame attached itself to families living in a 'moral' neighbourhood, and great anger was expressed at the time that it became known that an unmarried daughter was pregnant, this feeling quickly dissipated. Wyn Heywood illustrated this. When she learned that she was to have a baby whilst she was still single, her mother – a heavy drinker – erupted in fury. Yet 'rough' as her mother was, after the initial rage she stood by Heywood and showed great pride in her first grandchild. This left her daughter to wonder why, if her mother was so proud, she had thrown her disgrace in her face whilst she was expecting the baby. The explanation is to be found in a mother's concern for her children, no matter how they might shame her, and in her desire to maintain the unity of the family. Birmingham's welfare services urged Heywood to have her baby adopted; supported by her mother, she did not. This is a vital issue: amongst the moral poor, ties of blood were dominant over codes of behaviour. Even the emotionally-hard mother of Kathleen Dayuss who continually reminded her daughter of her disgrace, so much so that she was forced to leave home, was still the first person that Dayuss turned to when she needed someone to mind her child.

The adherence of the majority of women to the moral standards imposed by the matriarchy ensured that many girls were too scared to have sex before marriage. They feared that if they did and the fact became general knowledge, then their reputations would be besmirched and their characters would be slurred. In any poor neighbourhood there was a minority of young women who ignored and flouted convention. Kathleen Dayuss was friendly with such a girl, a 'bad lot', who was shunned by everybody (except, of course, her boyfriends), and in Studley Street there were two women who, before and after marriage, were well-known as being 'free and easy' with their favours, and who were, accordingly, the subject of much disapproving gossip. However, women such as these were distinguished by their paucity, at least in the public demonstration of their lack of adherence to respectable behaviour. As Alice Foley explained, the poor held to a fairly conventional, if unexplored, moral code. If any girl in her group was suspected of 'going out' with a married man, then she was usually due for a 'telling off' by her companions, whilst those few culprits who lived 'tally' (unmarried) were never accepted. Edith Hall emphasised the intensity with which the belief was held that sex before marriage and with someone other than a husband was morally wrong and something to be ashamed of. Amongst the munitions workers of the First World War, the canary girls of her title, it was understood that should any of their boyfriends 'try anything on', then they would expect to get their face slapped.

Prostitution, then, was certainly not a viable alternative means of earning money for a girl or woman from a poverty-stricken family which, although it might have been regarded as 'rough' by the rest of society, considered itself respectable according to the mores of the urban poor. Many writers had the impression that low earnings and unemployment were amongst the causes of prostitution, and for those women who cared little for their reputations, it is indeed likely that economic necessity was the main reason for their resort to it as a way in which they could ensure their survival. However, for the majority of girls in the period 1880–1939, such a reaction to their impoverishment was unthinkable. Any job, no matter how dirty, monotonous and ill-paid, was preferable to prostitution, and the abhorrence of it as a way of making money was probably responsible for the hard-working reputation of widows. Indeed, out of a fear that they would be thought 'fair game' and would become the subject of scandal, widows were likely to remarry. In fact, the frequency of remarriages amongst the poor was a matter for comment by M. E. Loane. It must be mentioned, nevertheless, that whilst prostitutes were figures of much disapprobation in lower-working-class neighbourhoods, in their everyday lives the poor could be tolerant of this type of dissident. This attitude of 'live and let live' is summed up by the phrase 'there but for the grace of God go I', which several of my women interviewees from highly moral backgrounds used when talking of local prostitutes and 'loose' women. They led lives which were morally wrong and 'dirty', but they were their lives and no-one else's. As Roberts said of women who gave up prostitution and married, whilst they were not accepted by the local community, they were tolerated.

Prostitutes, as with the women of the 'low' of the poor, were those who were most likely to attempt some form of primitive contraception in the form of home-made pessaries of lard or margarine and flour, or they might use a small piece of oiled sponge with tapes attached to it. The moral and the respectable shunned these devices, that is if they were aware of them. Instead, they placed their faith in the misguided belief that the longer they suckled their babies the less likely were their chances of becoming pregnant once again. It was common in poor quarters to see infants as old as two and three sucking at their mothers' breasts. Barrier forms of contraception which were increasingly popular amongst educated sections of society remained almost unheard of amongst the urban poor right through the 1920s and 1930s. Books, such as *Married Love* by Marie Stopes, which explained about contraception made little impression on them. In 1924 Dr Robertson could still state that birth-control had a greater effect on the skilled of the working class than it had on the poor. Wyn Heywood exemplified the ignorance of many women; on one occasion during the Second World War when her husband was home on leave, he took a packet out of his pocket. He explained to his wife, who thought he held a packet of Beecham's Powders, that it contained sheaths, the use of which he had to explain to her. There is little doubt that the armed services played a great role in educating the poor into the use of this form of contraceptive, as oral evidence also confirms. Yet the two decades before the 1939–45 war did witness a dramatic decline in the birth-rate in poor neighbourhoods and this can be attributed mostly to the increasingly open assertion of their independence by younger married women. No longer were they prepared to acquiesce in the supposed ascendancy of the male. They wanted to be overtly recognised in their position of power and in their freedom of action. A man's right to have sex whenever he demanded it was questioned more and more by many of the new generation of women (although not all). They were not prepared to have their lives ruined and their health impaired by the bearing of large numbers of children. My oral testimony is replete with phrases which hint at the increasing practice of coitus interruptus and even sexual abstinence, and that of Elizabeth Roberts seems to substantiate this. Phrases like 'I never had what med 'em' and 'I told him he could have 'em himself if he wanted more' indicate the new spirit of open equality, as do those such as 'my husband was not lustful' and 'my husband was not highly-sexed'.

For older women, and the more conservative and less strident of the young, however, there remained throughout the period 1880–1939 only one way in which they could successfully limit their families. Abortions lay in their own power and were not dependent on the consideration or lack of it of a husband. Dr Robertson inveighed against the widespread resort to abortion in 1905, but by 1916 Dr Roth estimated that there were four abortions to every one still-birth, of which there were 3·05% per 1,000 live births. In 1936 an Abortion Law Reform Association

Conference reported that from a sample of 3,000 women invest-igated by a prominent gynaecologist in Birmingham, thirty five per cent had at least one abortion. Robert Roberts recalled that, in the Edwardian era, newspapers were full of advertise-ments for abortifacients which were disguised as medicines suitable for removing obstructions. There existed many other, less expensive ways in which a wife could hope to abort a pregnancy and most consisted of drinking a mixture: penny royal syrup; aloes; gin; water in which pennies had been boiled, and others. Additionally, a woman might resort to violent activity; purchasing pills from a chemist or an aborti-facient for animals from a vet, or sitting over a bowl in which slippery elm was placed which was supposed to draw out the foetus. Amongst the poor it was believed that a woman had to be desperate to seek an end to her pregnancy and a curious distinction arose in the minds of some between a natural miscarriage and an abortion. To induce the former was not regarded as morally wrong, especially if it was early in pregnancy and brought on by a concoction. However, an abortion was seen as immoral, the resort – as a Birmingham woman believed – of 'hoity toity pieces' who had gone off with men before they were married. It was felt that these were the ones who would pay an abortionist or use a knitting needle themselves. Drinking 'something' did not seem as related to terminating a pregnancy as did the brutal use of knitting and crochet needles which, in effect, murdered the baby. Mary Chamberlain also noted this distinction, observing that most working-class women did not see it as wrong to induce a miscarriage before the baby had quickened. Whether inducing a miscarriage or an abortion, both were the solitary decision of a wife more aware of financial problems than a husband. They were also two of only a few ways in which a woman could control her own body, although both could prove fatal, as with the case cited by Gwendolen Freeman:

One morning, Alfred Benny went out leaving his wife energetically cleaning the floor. He returned from work to find her in bed and dying. The cause? Why, another baby, of course, and she hadn't wanted it and she had taken something. That is always happening in the lane. Things had gone wrong. She died that night. And he had not even known the other child was coming.[28]

In relation to the death of children, mention must be made of overlaying, or accidental smothering. Few households of the poor possessed a cot. Some might have a chest of drawers, one drawer of which was laid on the floor and an infant placed in it, but in the majority of families most babies slept between their mother and father. This practice, called in 1907 by Dr Robertson a very natural indiscretion, obviously led to deaths by accidental suffocation. Some of the middle class, however, saw in this not only the neglect of the poor but also their callousness. They felt that parents deliberately suffocated their babies so as to claim the burial insurance for them. The evidence does not bear this out, nor does it justify the assertion that the deaths were due to drunkenness. In 1920 there were twenty-seven cases of overlaying in Birmingham. In all but two instances, the families were said to be respectable and sober persons. There were, in all probability, a few cases of overlaying over the years in which the suffocating was deliberate: the Coroner's Reports for Birmingham intimated that this was particularly likely if a child was illegitimate. However, mass murder of their young by the poor is a charge irreconcilable with both the statistical and qualitative evidence. Mrs Liddel thought that the one softening influence left to the poor amidst a life stripped of everything that lent it charm was their love of their little children. Reginald Bray expressed the opinion in Masterman's book that there must have been something great in the lives of the children of the poor, something worthy of admiration, to cause the spontaneity of affection that was evident in them. Even Patterson believed that, whilst they were dragged up by their mothers, there was little cruelty and perhaps too much kindness in their upbringing.

There were parents who were overly violent in their correction of their children; there were those who were unmindful of the dangers posed by open fires and pots of boiling water (accidents from both these caused a number of deaths each year amongst children of the poor), and there were those parents who were deliberately inattentive to the physical as well as the emotional needs of their children. These latter were most evident in the districts of the 'low' of the poor where family life was not the dominant force it was in settled areas. In parts of the parish of St Laurence, the Reverend T. J. Bass believed sottishness and sensuality went together, and there is much to justify his observation. In *Hope in Shadowland*, he provided an example of the detestation of moral values evident in that small section of the lower working class who lived without any. A Mrs Brown, a mother with three children, attended afternoon meetings at his church and her quiet, silent character became a reproach to her neighbours. As a result, one of her children's spectacles were broken, her door was smashed in and finally she herself was beaten up by three men. Mrs Brown had the courage to summons her assailants who were, as a result, imprisoned. The wrath of her neighbours at her temerity was such that she and her family were forced to leave their house.

It was amongst the degenerate of the poor described by the Reverend Bass that the heinous sin, as the moral poor regarded it, of a father molesting his children was most likely to take place. Official figures do not exist which can adequately quantify the extent to which this occurred, given the hidden nature of the crime – hidden not only from the law but also, in a settled community, from the ire of neighbours. Bass was in no doubt about the 'contamination' of the young which took place in parts of his parish. He was no castigator of the lower working class; indeed he admired many of their characteristics and proved a staunch champion in defending them against the slurs of their detractors in the middle class. It would be foolish, therefore, to dismiss his observation that in deprived, and depraved, quarters of his parish, criminal offences against children were common, and that promiscuous family life led to child profligacy and licentiousness. Dr Hill was of the opinion that this was induced by the environment of the poor, believing that the sleeping arrangements in some poor households were prejudicial to morals. He based his assertion on the fact that brothers and sisters, and parents and children, often slept in the same bedroom, perhaps with just a curtain to separate the sections in which each slept.

It was this kind of environmental factor which fostered the charge that sexual immorality was more common amongst the poor than it was amongst other sections of society. Indeed, in an article entitled, 'A study of Victorian prostitution and venereal disease', that belief led E. M. Sigsworth and T. J. Wyke to suppose that prostitution was less commercialised amongst the working class, precisely because working-class men had little need to purchase what was freely available. Although this article referred mainly to the 1850s and 1860s, a period well before the full emergence of settled communities and the hidden matriarchy, this accusation has implications for the years of this study. I would argue strongly that only in the minority of families who were seen as already immoral by the poor were living conditions likely to affect sexual behaviour. My own oral evidence, and that of Elizabeth Roberts in particular, would support this rebuttal. It emphasises the innocence of each other's bodies that many children of both sexes had. Moreover, as children grew older and became teenagers, boys and their fathers would often sleep in one bedroom or downstairs, whilst girls and their mothers shared the use of the other bedroom. It is interesting that this separation of the sexes also usually signalled the end of sexual relations between husbands and wives and thus the welcome end of childbearing for a woman.

A father who was bent on assaulting his children sexually was likely to do so, irrespective of sleeping arrangements. The poor cannot be regarded as a section in which was inherent all that was an anathema to society as a whole. Nor can they be seen as totally free from the taints of that society. Child abuse and incest were present amongst the urban poor, just as they probably were in more prosperous sections of society. The reasons why they were more noticeable amongst the lower working class was simply that the poor were the subject of studies and visits in a way that the affluent were not. Incest was a serious contravention of the moral code of the poor, and naturally those who were involved in incestuous relationships did not proclaim the fact. Yet, in the close neighbourhoods of the poor where privacy was like an unattainable oasis, it was known that certain families were shamed by its presence. Robert Roberts mentions families such as these, and Catherine Cookson wrote of the attempts her uncle made to have sex with her mother, his half-sister. A Birmingham woman recalled that when she left home in the late 1920s she went to live with her aunt, her father's sister. However, she soon had to leave for fear of her uncle who was 'interfering' with his children. The punishment of men such as this was usually ostracisation, as we have seen, although the belief persisted that where incidents of incest were blatant, then neighbours would give the man 'a bloody good hiding' and hold his head under the communal stand-pipe whilst he was doused in cold water. It must also be borne in mind that fathers were not the only men who could try to molest children. A woman from Paddington recollected that the vicar of her parish church regularly tried to put his hand up her skirt, with the result that she was afraid to go into the vestry with him alone. Wyn Heywood remembered that, when she was about eleven, a man who was delivering coal put his hands inside her knickers. When her mother was told, she grabbed a knife and ran to the man's house screaming that she would kill him.

A final point needs to be made relating to the ill-treatment of children and the attitudes of the urban poor. In the sunken parts of the parish of St Laurence, the children of the respectable were as likely to be the targets of victimisation as were their parents. In contrast, in the settled neighbourhoods of the poor where the power of the matriarchy was marked, the neglected children of the deliberately uncaring minority became the responsibility of the whole community. Children of the respectable might be admonished not to play with them because of their dirtiness (an instruction always ignored) but adults did not allow the physical needs of the neglected children to pass unnoticed. An example of this is provided in the Studley Street locality of Birmingham during the 1930s:

Old M never looked after her kids, you know. I mean they was terrible, they was. There was one poor little thing . . . and our Granny used to go mad and she used to leave her in the garden and the poor little thing used to be crying, it was 'ungry, wringing, soaking wet . . . Our Gran couldn't stand it no more and she went and took the babbi out the pram and our Granny went mad at M and she let her have it right, left and centre . . . The thing was her used to get drunk and her used to go to bed with blokes and leave the kids. I can see that babbi in an old pram in the garden up against the wall, and the poor little thing had been there for hours. Now there was one thing about Studley Street. You could say the people was rough, alright. Now, if anybody was being cruel to children the neighbours'd fetch the bleedin' parents out or whoever, and stick their bleedin' heads under the tap and give 'em a good pasting . . . They couldn't stand cruelty to children. That's one thing they couldn't stand . . . Our Gran, blimey, she never had much but when there was some kids crying for bread, our Granny'd fetch 'em in and gie 'em a piece.[29]

Jerry White has emphasised that, in Campbell Bunk too, women's support networks were concerned with the protection of children and young adults.

Chapter five

Fighting back

Those women of the urban poor who successfully prevented the fall of their families into total indigence and utter hopelessness were united by a spirit of determination and an indomitable character. They were also fighters. This trait was noticeable as much in their personal relations as it was in their struggle against poverty. Nowhere was it more evident than in their dealings with their husbands.

When discussing relations between a husband and wife, it needs to be borne in mind that amongst the poor there was a small proportion of couples united not by a legal contract or religious ceremony, but by faithfulness to each other. Dr Robertson noticed their existence in Birmingham, as did Lady Bell in Middlesbrough. In any discussion on marriage, therefore, these couples should not be omitted because of the irregular nature of their union but should be included because of the stability of their relationships. The poor married for a variety of reasons. Some sought to escape from an unhappy home life or believed their independence would increase away from the control of their parents, and so eagerly anticipated marriage. Others drifted into a relationship, accepting married life as an inevitable stage in their existence. Many women were forced into marriage by the pressures of lower-working-class society; a woman might be expecting a baby and needed to marry to retain her respectability, or she might be afraid of becoming a spinster and not having children. Despite the fears of childbirth, and its dangers, and despite motherhood often appearing as a bane, it was a rare woman of the urban poor who did not want children at all. Widows and widowers often remarried for company, as did bachelor sons when their mothers had died. Yet, as Patterson observed, the real cause of most marriages in London's dockland, as in other poor neighbourhoods, was love. The depth of that love might vary and it was this which could lead to the embitterment of many relationships in the face of hardship. Poverty made some couples, usually those who had been deepest in love, cling all the more closely to each other, but with many it placed severe strains on their affection with the result that love could be replaced by a feeling of exasperation with a partner.

The harsh reality of living in poverty swiftly and insensitively thrust aside the fleeting dreams of a newly-married couple; as Patterson said, a wedding seemed to end all nudging and giggling. Kathleen Dayuss could never remember her parents kissing, only sniping at each other on the occasions when they were on speaking terms. Many couples were the same. Yet beneath an exterior soured by disillusionment and weariness rather than dislike, the embers of affection lay waiting to be ignited once more in many partners. A couple from Birmingham who married in 1912 illustrated this point. They fought with each other from the day they married – the husband actually blacked his wife's eye as they left the church. This man was intensely jealous of his wife. He would buy her a new bonnet regularly when they were first married and take her out for a walk. Yet if he thought another man had looked at her he would storm home, throw the bonnet on the fire and beat his partner. In time she began to retaliate and it would seem that this marriage was typical of a union amongst the lower working class that was characterised by violence and was regarded by many commentators as the norm in poor neighbourhoods. So it was, and it was probably also typical in the undercurrent of unspoken and intangible love that ran beneath the surface of the marriage, as a letter written by the husband in 1964 to his wife in hospital indicated:

Just a few lines to you my dear to let you know that you will be surprised when you come home for the traffic down the street. I shall be very glad when (you) come home as your company will be more than anythink else. My dearest I am trying to come up on Wednesday night with Winnie. I would have been up there every night if I had been a bit

younger. As I am very anxious to get you home. I remain your affectionate
   Husband.[30]

The poor were not incapable of love, but loving was less easy when a family lived in poverty.

   A continual sniping at each other by man and wife was common to most marriages. So too was the violence that was evident in many lower-working-class unions. As early as 1855 an American who wrote to *The Birmingham Journal* voiced the opinion that the women of the poor were made to be the sport of ignorant oafs, to be battered and kicked by them and to be cudgelled into submission. The Reverend Bass also believed that, after constable-baiting, the next most popular 'pastime' of many husbands was wife-beating. This was a less exciting but nonetheless satisfying form of aggression because wives seldom prosecuted their husbands for causing them bodily harm. Whilst accepting the general prevalence of wife-beating in all poor neighbourhoods, it is necessary to recognise a difference between that violence which was accepted by lower-working-class society as normal within a marriage, and that which was not. A very subtle distinction lay between the two, and the fine shades of difference obvious to the poor were unclear to outsiders. Abnormal violence flourished in the unsettled, sunken districts where women were little respected and matriarchs notable by their absence. It took the form of vicious beatings from pitiless husbands who sought through their savagery to dominate their wives totally and to effect their complete subjugation. Mrs Liddel wrote of a woman who preferred to spend the night sleeping with her child in the outdoor wash-house rather than risk the dangers of home with a drunken and violent husband. Another wife regularly hid under a bed when her husband came home as it was his habit to kick her round the room with his thick, nailed boots when he was drunk. The parish of St Laurence provided the Reverend Bass with many similar examples: a wife whose husband jumped on her and crushed in part of her skull; women who were never free of a black eye or bruised ribs, and the following horrendous account of a wife who came to his lodge seeking help for her children and herself:

Last evening my husband came home and asked me for some money as
he wanted to get a drink: I had none. I had spent my last shilling in
buying a second-hand pair of boots for the child. He swore at me and
tried to lay hold of the child that he might get the boots off his feet and
take them to the pawn office, but I snatched the child from his arms and
we fought . . . Early in the morning, when all was still . . . he lit the fire
and boiled the kettle . . . Some little time elapsed. I felt a sudden shock
all over me, he had taken a saucepan of boiling water and thrown it
over my naked legs and body, and before I could get up he jumped on
me, then he took the warm ashes from the fire and rubbed it into my
sweating flesh, then he held me by the throat, dug his nails into my
neck and tried to strangle me, but I shrieked and he became terrified
and ran away.[31]

This woman, supported by the vicar, differed from most wives
who were subjected to this type of brutal assault. Her husband
was arrested and sentenced to five years' imprisonment for his
cruelty. Bass reported that the woman successfully earned her
own living following his incarceration. Yet most wives in 'low'
districts had to stay with their husbands. Firstly, the cost of
divorce was prohibitive to the lower working class, although
the twentieth century did see the introduction of a Poor
Person's Divorce. Secondly, the cost of a separation order was
also often unattainable for a woman whose income was low and
whose weekly expenses were high. At the turn of the century an
order cost 10s 6d but, in the case of the woman whose head was
partly caved in, her earnings from wood-chopping were only six
shillings a week. Finally, there was another reason which, much
oral evidence indicates, was as important as the financial ones,
especially in the case of wife-beating in more settled areas;
lower-working-class society expected a wife to stay with her
husband, no matter what his character. As one Birmingham
woman said, as you made your bed you were expected to lie on it.
Another agreed, stating that, when two people married, they
became committed to each other and that if either had returned
to their parents they would have been told to go back where they
belonged. This was especially the case where there were
children involved. The great majority of wives would never
abandon their children, whatever the conditions they suffered,
and if they tried to leave their husbands and take the children
with them, it was widely believed that there was nowhere they
could find refuge. It was thought that no-one would offer
lodging to a wife along with children, and the only alternative

was regarded as the workhouse, which was a place dreaded by all the poor. Yet many wives of the urban poor were independent; they often supported their families out of their own wages. It is inconceivable in the light of evidence from this study that strong women who were financially able and free in their actions could not find accommodation if they left their husbands, and could not also support themselves and their children if they did so. The example of widows, abandoned wives and the woman quoted by Bass would seem to justify this assertion. In reality, the oral evidence does not argue against this but emphasises the acceptability of violence within marriage in settled areas so long as that violence remained limited by certain restrictions on its level. Fighting between man and wife was regarded by the poor as normal behaviour; it was part of life and was no excuse for a marriage to break up.

That is not to say that, even in the communities of the moral of the poor, assaults by a husband on his wife could not be savage. Wyn Heywood provided an example of this. Her husband regarded her only as 'a kid-making machine' who was there to satisfy his lust. He continually raped and beat her, so severely on one occasion that one of her eardrums burst, causing permanent deafness in that ear. Eventually, Heywood could take no more punishment, mental as well as physical, and left her home, her community and her city, and abandoned her children. This action provides further proof that a man's violence had to be particularly brutal for his wife to leave him, for, as Kathleen Dayuss found when she put her children into care for their own good, desertion of her children made her a terrible woman, the 'wust' in the district. It is difficult to argue for, let alone define, acceptable levels of violence, yet it is obvious that, in an unconscious way, the poor managed to do this. Grace Foakes recalled that many women in her community – which she described as having a great sense of values regarding moral behaviour – were given a 'good hiding' by their husbands. The following day they would emerge with black eyes and swollen faces, yet would not utter a word against their partners and woe betide anyone else who did. A code of conduct, strange to us today in its implications, was adhered to. As a Birmingham man said, you never interfered with a husband and wife fighting, no matter how bloody the battle might sound.

However, as John Douglas also commented, if a man other than
a husband hit a wife, then he would be subject to the fury not
just of her partner but of the other men in the community. This
code included a lack of malice between a husband and wife after
a fight was over, as Alice Foley observed, and it also ensured
that, in some circumstances, black eyes became almost a status
symbol. As the son of an Edwardian mother recalled, in his poor
locality in Birmingham a black eye was worn like a medal, with
a sense of pride; wives compared totals of the number they had
received as they sat drinking together in the beer house. His
own mother had received twenty-two in eleven years of marriage, a figure which enhanced her prestige amongst her
neighbours.

Acceptable violence could still be highly fierce; it did not stop
at a push and a shove, or a slap across the face. One Birmingham
woman recalled the fighting in her home in the 1920s:

Our Dad was on the boats at eight, working his guts out. And I'm sure
he med our Mom pay for it, I'm sure. I've seen that lady have some
beltings. Our Nance was born with black eyes, the way he'd belted her.
Then her jumped the bedroom winder when her was having Winnie 'cus
he was belting her . . . Even the midwife's summonsed out Dad. Nurse
Caddock. Belting our Mom. I don't know which babbi it was. And the
vicar summonsed him . . . It got squashed. He said he'd alter his ways. A
man had nine points of the law then . . . Oh, he worn't one on his own!
Oh no! Every man in Whitehouse Street was like it.[32]

This man, a good provider and kind to his children, was the same
person who wrote the letter to his wife in 1964. His personality
exemplified the contrary character of most lower-working-class
men, and his family life indicated the standards of behaviour
acceptable amongst the poor.

It is tempting in all this to see the wives of the urban poor as
the victims of the aggression of men, passively receiving their
beatings because that was life. In the case of thousands of
women, nothing could be further from the truth. Working wives
especially developed a physical strength comparable to that of
many men. Their jobs demanded it, and even those women who
were not in employment carried out strenuous household tasks
which required of them a force and vigour not necessary in
the women of the more affluent sections of society. This is
particularly true of the period before the First World War, but in

the 1930s numbers of women remained who retained a physical hardness. Helen Forrester observed them in Liverpool. She described one woman of this mould as a 'scarefying looking person' who was hugely fat and had legs like iron-clad pillars. In the youngster's view, this woman was 'outlandishly fierce looking'. Kathleen Dayuss's mother never walked like a woman should (as the rest of English society thought); she seemed to stride along, taking big steps, with her back straight and her head held high. She could also fight like a man. On one occasion, whilst on a 'holiday' for women and children spent hop-picking in the country, she and the other women became involved in a fight with some local men. Dayuss described how her mother punched one man in the stomach with 'a right and a left' and followed this with a kick in his groin, at which her opponent fell to the ground, defeated. That was not the end of the fight for her mother. She stepped over the prostrate man so as to help the other women in their struggles, which left Dayuss without any doubt that her mother was enjoying herself.

This kind of toughness in women was often learned early. Forrester's brother told her that she was lucky not to have to go to his new school in the slums, as even the girls fought. Both the woman from Paddington and the eldest daughter of the Birmingham family of twelve were taught to box by their fathers, and, as the latter recalled, with a brother eleven months older and one ten months younger, she had to learn to take her own part. Fights between women – usually the result of squabbles over children – could be as vicious as between man and wife, as Forrester and Mrs Liddel described, but importantly in the vicar's wife's description, she emphasised that women used their fists as well as their nails. Charles Booth, in his second volume, mentioned a strong woman who lived in one of the poorest streets, Shelton Street. Clean in room and person, she was also desperate with fist and tongue when drunk. The image of women fighting like cats, scratching and snarling at each other and pulling at each other's hair is an incorrect one. Women of the urban poor fought as did men, with their fists, supplemented if necessary by their nails, and were admired for doing so by their communities. Another Birmingham man recalled:

... the old girl could fight like, better than a mon ... Tek anybody on.
Dad'd been to work one Saturday morning. He had his dinner, went up
to The Wrexham to have a drink. And he hadn't been out long when he
come back and all his lip was bleedin'. And the old girl says,
    'Who's done that?'
There used to be a gang in The Wrexham, about seven or eight handed.
So Mom says to me,
    'Come with me son.'
We went up to The Wrexham and when we got to the corner she opened
the door and she looked in ... There were two brothers and this one as
hit the old mon he come the door and he come out onto the pavement.
And mother hit him. Bump. Down he went. And he wouldn't get up to
have another one. And her went to the door again to pull his brother
out. But he wouldn't come out when he'd seen what had happened. Her
was never afraid of the old mon.[33]

Women like this, and like Kathleen Dayuss's mother, were
not exceptional in lower-working-class neighbourhoods. The
wives of the urban poor lived in a highly physical environment
and had to learn to fight, sooner rather than later, if they were to
survive. If they had not learned before they married, many
learned after. It would be wrong to see these women as weak and
defenceless. They fought back against their husbands and could
be equally strong and aggressive. Jerry White recited a story
told him by a policeman which exemplified this. One Sunday in
the 1930s the constable was walking along 'The Bunk' when a
little girl came running over to him. She was crying and asked
him to come and see what 'mummy' had done to dad. On entering
the family's home, the policeman found the husband lying
unconscious, spread-eagled on his back. Standing over him was
his grim-faced wife, holding the remains of a chamber-pot. In
reply to the question of what had happened, the woman replied
that her husband had come home drunk and declared that he
was 'the king of the castle'. In response to this assertion of male
supremacy, his wife simply decided to 'crown' him! M. E. Loane
gave other examples of 'doughty champions of the supremacy of
women' who beat their husbands for coming home more foolish
than when they went out.

Women were also more likely to be aware of tactics in their
fights with men, and one which many used to good effect was to
enlist the support of their sons. The Birmingham mother of
twelve remembered that her father stopped fighting with her
mother after the family's two eldest brothers had warned him

off, and Walter Allen described a similar occurrence in his novel. The alertness of mind of which Anna Martin spoke was another useful asset in a wife who was determined not to be made subservient to her husband. Roberts recounted the apocryphal story of the husband who, when he was too drunk to be able to resist, was tied up by his wife and beaten senseless. This action successfully ensured his future sobriety. The tale had many similarities with reality. A Birmingham man remembered that the women in his neighbourhood would often 'belt' their husbands when the men were drunk and unable to fight back properly, whilst a woman from the same city recalled that if her parents had rowed before her father went out for a drink, her mother would watch the clock and, a few minutes after closing time, would blow the gas out and stand behind the door. When her husband came in she would then attack him. Strong women did not have to wait till a man was incapacitated by drink to fight back; if the occasion demanded it, then they would battle with their men sober as well. George Acorn's parents fought without quarter or mercy given on either side and A. P. Jasper's mother once gave her husband the biggest hiding her son believed any woman could possibly give a man. This was caused because she found out that he had regularly spent on drink the money she had left at home for her children, with which to buy food for their dinner. Mrs Jasper was described as having two arms that were like legs of mutton and when the men of the family saw her rolling her sleeves up, then they knew it was time to placate her. A woman like this was as able to dominate her family physically as much as she was financially and emotionally.

Physical violence was not the only means available to a woman to fight back against a husband who was inconsiderate of the needs of the rest of the family. Roberts recalled with relish how one man was discontented with the fillings of the sandwiches his wife made him for work. He felt that they should consist of items of food to which the family budget, as his wife knew, could not extend. After a violent row on one occasion, he found the next day that his lunch consisted of the rent book between two slices of bread! Another wife, who stood six feet tall and weighed nineteen stone, inverted a plate of hash over her drunken husband's head when he finally decided to return home from the pub, whilst one woman cured her husband of staying out late drinking with his friends by giving the meal he turned down on his return to the dog. As Roberts so rightly stated, not every woman accepted the almighty male with subservience and tears; not all of them called their husbands master.

Lady Bell believed that many women of the working class went on from day to day without taking part in the wider life outside them, without being in the least interested in any public question. Helen Forrester was of the same opinion twenty-five years later, declaring that one of the penalties paid for being poor was that of being cut off from the rest of the world. It is true that the great majority of the women of the lower working class withdrew into the closed communities of the poor, shunning society outside and evincing a distinct lack of curiosity about anything which did not directly affect them or their families. This seclusion was not a sign of defeat; the women of the poor recognised that their strength and power lay within their own neighbourhoods and that, away from them, this would disappear. Realism was a distinguishing feature of these women. They were aware of the daunting challenge which poverty threw down, they recognised the difficulties in staving off its worst excesses, they were fully cognisant of the dangers inherent in slum life and they knew, above all, the responsibility which lay upon them to secure the survival of their family in a clean and moral way. Women of the urban poor were realists but not fatalists. This is not to say that they did not recognise that little they could do could in any way guarantee their future. However, whilst they believed that 'what will be, will be', the majority of them did not passively submit to all that happened to them and see it as inevitable. If they had, their poverty would have become destitution and their morality would have degenerated into immorality. The choice which thousands of women of the urban poor made was to act against what an unjust society had decreed should be their lot. They fought back with vigour and tenacity. They did not surrender.

This book has explained the means whereby this battle was fought. The greatest asset lower-working-class women had was themselves; their allies, each other; their support, the love and devotion of their children. As A. P. Jasper wrote, it took a strong character like his mother to keep the family on an even keel. That strength was not a quality which was lacking in thousands of women for whom fate had decreed that they should live in the slums of the towns and cities of England. Their physical strength was ensured by the arduous nature of their housework and their employment and, as Ellen Ross has stated, their work in particular ensured that they would be neither lady-like nor deferential to their men. The culture of maleness which strove to keep women at home struggled unsuccessfully to impose itself on the urban poor, amongst whom women remained economically as well as emotionally significant. The mutual devotion of mothers and children ensured that this latter would be so; it was this which gave to mothers their inner strength. As Patterson himself stated, despite all his qualifications as to the success of mothers of the urban poor, they were the hope and soul of the home life of their families: 'blessed are the mothers for they shall be much loved'. This devotion of their children, together with the dominance of blood ties in settled communities and the importance of the extended family and the neighbourhood, meant that mothers would control their communities. It cannot be disputed that middle-class philanthropy and municipal activity helped to improve the environment and the health of the poor, no matter how marginally. More important, however, for the daily lives of the lower working class was the crucial role of mothers. This they extended through their relationships with each other, so that in most neighbourhoods the poor governed and controlled themselves through the power and influence wielded by mothers.

The social repercussions of the First World War did have significant effects on women who lived in the slums, and this was especially obvious in their new assertiveness. During the war and with so many men away fighting, the control women had over life in the slums became open for all to see. In many respects it was shown that their men were not needed; women were doing men's jobs and, for the first time, they were openly in control of their own destinies. With their return, men found it harder to reimpose the old *status quo* whereby overt power was in their hands and covert power was in the hands of the women. The war shattered the myth of male dominance and enabled the hidden matriarchy to emerge, and at the same time it ensured that men would have to come to terms with this new situation. The most apparent effect on the lives of men was that sex was no longer an act in which women acquiesced, whatever their own feelings. Many women decided that they would no longer give what they did not want to, with the result that men had to change. In a host of ways, young women were determined to proclaim their freedom. They began to wear make-up; they abandoned their shawls for fashionable clothes; they started to drink in public houses with their boyfriends or girlfriends; they danced and went to the pictures to escape into a dream world, and, most importantly, they decided to limit the size of their families. Men had little option but to follow along in their wake, adapting themselves in a way their fathers would never have contemplated doing.

Yet, whilst it is undeniable that many euphoric changes were taking place in the lives of the women of the urban poor, other vital aspects of their lives remained the same. The most pervasive of these was their poverty. The impoverishment of the lower working class did not dissipate with social change; it remained to haunt and hinder the attempts of women at improvement. The effects of poverty were everywhere apparent. So too were its symbols: the pawnshop; the money-lender; the 'strap' at the corner shop; a poor education, and ill-paid jobs and unemployment. This meant that the new generation of women, in spite of crucial differences, still led their lives much as their mothers and grandmothers had before the First World War, and indeed were to do so right up to the early 1960s. They still could not afford to be dejected, dispirited or defeated; they still needed an inborn energy that no amount of child-birth, no end of hard work and no limit to the ceaseless fight against privation could quench. Some may have fallen by the wayside, others may have lost any gaiety they might have possessed, and who could blame them? The majority, however, who succeeded to a greater or lesser extent were distinguished by pride, by determination and by independence. Poverty could not defeat them, men could not command them and society could not subdue them. Hard work remained their lot and, however much society changed, one fact remained unalterable: women of the urban poor worked all their lives.

Notes

1 *Pictures of The People. Drawn by One of Themselves*, Number IV, 'How they live', 12 June 1871.
2 George Gissing, *The Nether World*, first published 1889, Everyman edition, 1973, p. 130.
3 Benny Green, introduction to Clarence Rook, *The Hooligan Nights*, first published 1899, Oxford University Press edition, 1979, p. viii.
4 Robert Roberts, *The Classic Slum*, Penguin edition, 1973, p. 124.
5 Women's Group on Public Welfare, *Our Towns*, cited in Arthur Collis and Vera E. Poole, *These Our Children*, 1950, p. 10.
6 C. Chinn Interviews, No.28, Mrs L. Baker, pp. 18–20.
7 Jack London, *The People of The Abyss*, first published 1903, Journeyman edition, 1977, p. 114.
8 C. Chinn Interviews, No. 8, Mr T. Parker, pp. 1–16.
9 C. Chinn Interviews, No. 29, Mrs L. Perry, p. 9.
10 C. Chinn Interviews, No. 30, Mrs M. Rose, pp. 12–13.
11 C. Chinn Interviews, No. 32, Mrs W. Martin, pp. 2–3.
12 C. Chinn Interviews, No. 2, Mr Walter Chinn, pp. 38–55.
13 City of Birmingham Health Department, *Report on the Industrial Employment of Married Women and Infantile Mortality*, 1909, p. 19.
14 C. Chinn Interviews, No. 30, Mrs M. Rose, p. 16.
15 C. Chinn Interviews, No. 8, Mr T. Parker, pp. 18–19.
16 Jack Lannigan, in John Burnett (ed.), *Destiny Obscure. Autobiographies of Childhood Education and Family from the 1820s to the 1920s*, 1982, p. 99.
17 C. Chinn Interviews, No. 31, Mrs L. Walsh, p. 67.
18 C. Chinn Interviews, No. 2, Mr Walter Chinn, p. 2.
19 C. Chinn Interviews, No. 28, Mrs L. Baker, pp. 16–17.
20 *The Birmingham Daily Post*, Tuesday 1 January 1901. Article headed 'Drunkenness among women. Reported alarming increase'.
21 C. Chinn Interviews, No. 32, Mrs W. Martin, pp. 8–9.
22 C. Chinn Interviews, No. 31, Mrs L. Walsh, pp. 10–11.
23 C. Chinn Interviews, No. 2, Mr Walter Chinn, pp. 30–2.

24 C. Chinn Interviews, No. 2, Mr Walter Chinn, pp. 47–8.

25 C. Chinn Interviews, No. 30, Mrs M. Rose, pp. 14–15.

26 J. Cuming Walters, *Scenes in Slumland. Pen Pictures of the Black Spots in Birmingham*, Article No. 2, reprinted from *The Birmingham Daily Post*, 1901.

27 C. Chinn Interviews, No. 31, Mrs L. Walsh, p. 9.

28 Gwendolen Freeman, *The Houses Behind. Sketches of a Birmingham Back Street*, 1947, p. 16.

29 C. Chinn Interviews, No. 31, Mrs L. Walsh, pp. 11–12.

30 Letter from William Wood to his wife, Lilian, 13 April 1964.

31 Rev. T. J. Bass, *Tragedies of Life: Fragments of Today*, 1903, pp. 12–13.

32 C. Chinn Interviews, No. 29, Mrs L. Perry, pp. 2–3.

33 C. Chinn Interviews, No. 1, Mr Walter Chinn, pp. 49–50.

Sources

Oral evidence

All oral evidence I have used in this book, unless otherwise stated, is derived from eighty-five interviews I have in my archives at present. The following list names those whose testimony has been relevant to this study. It also gives their date of birth, their residence relevant to this book, the size of their family, and a brief outline of their family circumstances.

Lottie Ainley, née Stokes, Studley Street locality, one of six children by father's first marriage; father married three times; eighteen children. Father unemployed. Mrs Ainley's mother died when she was five and, as she was her grandmother's favourite, she was granny-reared on her paternal side until she married. Grandmother was charlady for the same middle-class family for many years. Local matriarch, known as Granny Stokes.

Lizzie Baker, 1912, Unett Street and Ladywood, Birmingham, five children in family. Father polisher, often unemployed. Mother Italian; she died when Lizzie was ten so that she was partly granny-reared until her father remarried. Left home at sixteen. Worked in a factory. Widowed with three children at the age of twenty-eight. Took in washing and cleaned the houses of better-off, local working-class families in Ladywood whilst on the parish. Neighbour minded children when she returned to work in a factory.

William Chinn, 1893, Studley Street locality, one of five children of whom two died in infancy, one as a result of a scalding from the water in the stew-pot. Father ex-regular army, then labourer who never earned more than eighteen shillings a week before 1914. Mother took in washing, then became wardrobe dealer, eventually renting own shop. Local matriarch known as Granny Chinn.

Walter Chinn, 1898, youngest of three surviving brothers. Fought in trenches at the age of sixteen and after war helped oldest brother, Alfred, with street bookmaking.

Violet Brown, née Chinn, 1925, Studley Street, only daughter by father's first marriage; mother died when she was two. Father local street bookie. Brought up by her father and particularly by her mother's youngest sister.

Buck Chinn, 1932, Studley Street, one of eight children by father's second marriage; one died in infancy. Mother left home when eldest child eleven. Father became 'father and mother' to children, helped by his daughter from his first marriage, his mother and his first wife's family.

Stella Couper, née Chinn, 1937, Studley Street locality, youngest daughter of second marriage; mother left whilst she was still a baby. Remembers that she was always attracted to the homes of the older women in Studley Street because she had no mother.

Florence Curtis, née Harris, 1903, Studley Street locality, one of thirteen children, of whom five died. Father upholsterer.

Gladys Davidson, née Matthews, 1926, Garrison Street, Garrison Lane. Youngest daughter of nine children, one died in infancy and one died aged sixteen. Father labourer at BSA.

Stan Doughty, 1907, Sparkbrook, Birmingham, one of five boys. Family thrust into poverty when father sacked for his part in the leadership in Birmingham of the 1919 police strike. Mother took in washing, family on parish and part-time jobs of children.

Sam Froggat, 1903, Studley Street locality, one of five children. Father wire-maker, mother widowed when Sam was ten and family moved to Saltley. Children had to help mother as best they could.

Carrie Griffiths, 1911, Studley Street locality, one of ten children. Father self-employed carter.

Lucy Ward, 1910, Studley Street locality. Younger sister of Carrie.

Celia Harris, 1913, Paddington, one of nine children living in two rooms. Father war pension from the First World War. Never gave his wife housekeeping. Consequently, she worked at whatever she could to earn money.

Billy Inchley, 1926, Studley Street, only child. Mother died when he was a baby and so he was granny-reared by her mother, Old Lady Snow. Her two sisters and their families also lived in the street. She was the local layer-out.

Katie Thomas, née James, 1921, Studley Street, one of four children by mother's first marriage. She then had four more children by her second husband.

Fred James, 1922, Studley Street. Father died of effects of gassing when Fred was a baby. Poorest family I have come across; lived, slept and cooked in one room. Mother took in washing to supplement parish and children earned money however they could. Depended for food on soup kitchens and mother's family who lived in the next street.

'Pony' Moore, 1909, Studley Street, one of seven children. Father unemployed for most of inter-war period, although his family was thought to be 'posh'. Mother an orphan raised by aunt; did not work. Consequently, the family was very poor and depended on the part-time and later full-time earnings of the children. Joined the navy to escape unemployment.

Maud Rose, née Moore, 1912, Studley Street. For most of the early 1930s was the only person in the household who worked.

Lil Nead, née Preston, 1913, Studley Street, eldest daughter of eleven children, three by her mother's first marriage. Two children died in infancy. Mother's first husband died. Father factory worker. Mother strong character. Children very close to her mother, Granny Carey.

Bill Preston, 1920, eldest son of mother's second marriage.

Teddy Parker, 1911, Studley Street, one of two brothers. Father horse-dealer who died when Teddy was two. Mother worked in local laundry and children partly brought up by her parents who lived in the same street.

Winston Remington, 1900, Studley Street locality, one of ten children. Father saddler, often unemployed. Family straddled the poverty line. Children had part-time jobs but mother did not.

Ted Sleath, 1908, Studley Street locality, one of six children. Father bricklayer and, for a short time, an unsuccessful street bookie. Mother worked in factory.

Lil Walsh, 1908, Studley Street locality, one of six children. Father killed in the First World War. Mother never remarried and supported family by working in a factory. Children spent a lot of time with her mother, Granny Carey.

Lil Perry, née Wood, 1914, Aston, Birmingham, eldest daughter of twelve children, of whom one died in infancy. Father labourer and unemployed for much of the 1920s. Refused to go on parish as too proud. Consequently, depended on mother's earnings from home work, the taking in of washing and charring. She laid out the dead and helped deliver babies. Known as Granny Wood.

George Wood, 1915, Aston, second eldest son of family. Left home to join army in 1931.

Winnie Martin, née Wood. One of younger daughters, brought up for a short time by better-off neighbour.

Sylvia Chinn, 1936, elder daughter of two of Lilian. Mother worked in factory so partly granny-reared, and like little mother to her sister eleven years younger.

I would like to acknowledge the help of Wendy Thwaite, whose interviews with Mr McKay and Mrs N. Thwaite – both from Lancashire – and with Mr Ted Norton – from London – have proven most useful. Information provided by the following people from the Studley Street locality has also been relevant: Wally Coates, Cathy Kench, Cathy oliver, Edna Turnbull, Mr Weake, Rita Whetton and Joycie White. I thank them for their help.

Manuscript sources

Allen, Dora, *My Earliest Recollections of Life at the Turn of the Century* (1968), City of Birmingham Central Reference Library, Local Studies Department.

City of Birmingham Coroner's Reports 1880–1914, City of Birmingham Central Reference Library, Archives Department.

Clifton Road Board School (Infants), Log Book 1878–96, City of Birmingham Central Reference Library, Archives Department.

Register of Marriages of St Barnabas' Church, Balsall Heath, Birmingham, 1905–14, City of Birmingham Central Reference Library, Archives Department.

Register of Marriages of St Paul's Church, Balsall Heath, Birmingham, 1905–14, City of Birmingham Central Reference Library, Archives Department.

The Educational Census Books of the City of Birmingham, City of Birmingham Central Reference Library, Archives Department.

Contemporary reports

A Handbook for Birmingham and the Neighbourhood (prepared for a meeting of the British Association for the Advancement of Science), Birmingham, 1913, City of Birmingham Central Reference Library, Local Studies Department.

Annual Reports of the Medical Officer of Health of Birmingham, 1880–1939, City of Birmingham Central Reference Library, Local Studies Department.

Birmingham Women's Settlement, Summer Lane, Annual Reports and Pamphlets 1905–25, City of Birmingham Central Reference Library, Local Studies Department.

City of Birmingham Education Committee, Central Care Committee, *Birmingham Trades for Women and Girls*, 1914, City of Birmingham Central Reference Library, Local Studies Department.

City of Birmingham Health Committee, *Report on the Industrial Employment of Married Women and Infantile Mortality*, Birmingham 1909, City of Birmingham Central Reference Library, Local Studies Department.

Muirhead, J. H., *Social Conditions in Provincial Towns*, No. 8, Birmingham, 1912, City of Birmingham Central Reference Library, Local Studies Department.

The Birmingham Ladies Union of Workers among Women and Girls, Conference 1890, Birmingham, 1891, City of Birmingham Central Reference Library, Local Studies Department.

Transactions of the National Association for the Promotion of Social Science, Birmingham, London, 1858, City of Birmingham Central Reference Library, Local Studies Department.

Press

The Balsall Heath Times
The Birmingham Daily Gazette

The Birmingham Daily Post
The Birmingham Journal
The Moseley and Kings Heath Journal

Working-class autobiographies and biographies

Acorn, George, *One of the Multitude, An Autobiography of a Resident of Bethnal Green*, London, 1911.

Burnett, John (ed.), *Useful Toil: Autobiographies of Working People from the 1820s to the 1920s*, London, 1974.

Burnett, John (ed.), *Destiny Obscure: Autobiographies of childhood, education and family from the 1820s to the 1920s*, London, 1982.

Chew, Doris Nield, *Ada Nield Chew: The Life and Writings of a Working Woman*, London, 1982.

Cookson, Catherine, *Our Kate. An Autobiography*, London, 1969, Corgi edition, 1986.

Dayuss, Kathleen, *Her People*. London, 1982.

Dayuss, Kathleen, *Where There's Life*, London, 1985.

Ezard, Edward, *Battersea Boy*, London, 1969.

Finn, Ralph L., *No Tears in Aldgate. An Autobiography*, Bath, 1963.

Foakes, Grace, *Between High Walls*, London, 1972.

Foakes, Grace, *My Part of The River*, London, 1974.

Foley, Alice, *A Bolton Childhood*, Manchester, 1973.

Forrester, Helen, *Twopence to Cross the Mersey*, Glasgow, 1981.

Forrester, Helen, *Liverpool Miss*, Glasgow, 1986.

Gamble, Rose, *Chelsea Child*, London, 1979.

Golding, Tom, *96 Years a Brummie, 1889–1986*, Birmingham, 1986.

Hall, Edith, *Canary Girls and Stockpots*, Luton, 1977.

Haw, G., *From Workhouse to Westminster: The Life Story of Will Crooks*, MP, London, 1909.

Heywood, Wyn, *My Mother's Story*, Middlesex, 1986.

Hobbs, May, *Born To Struggle*, London, 1973.

Jasper, A. P., *A Hoxton Childhood*, London, 1969.

Roberts, Robert, *A Ragged Schooling. Growing up in the Classic Slum*, Manchester, 1976.

Roberts, Robert, *The Classic Slum*, Manchester, 1978.

Rodaway, Angela, *A London Childhood*, London, 1960, Virago edition, 1985.

Samuel, Raphael, *East End Underworld: Chapters in The Life of Arthur Harding*, London, Boston and Henley, 1981.

Scannel, Dolly, *Mother Knew Best. An East End Childhood*, London, 1974.

Woodward, Kathleen, *Jipping Street*, first published in 1928, Virago edition, London, 1983.

Contemporary studies on the working class

Bass, Rev. T. J., *Everyday in Blackest Birmingham. Facts Not Fiction*, Birmingham, 1898.

Bass, Rev. T. J., *Hope in Shadowland*, Birmingham, 1903.

Bass, Rev. T. J., *Tragedies of Life – A Fragment of Today*, Birmingham, 1903.

Bass, Rev. T. J., *Down East amongst the Poorest*, Birmingham, 1904.

Bass, Rev. T. J., *Church Work among the Shadows. St Laurence Parish, Birmingham*, Birmingham, c.1913.

Bell, Lady, *At the Works: A Study of a Manufacturing Town*, London, 1911.

Besant, Walter, *East London*, London, 1901.

Black, Clementina (ed.), *Married Women's Work*, London, 1915.

Booth, Charles, *Life and Labour of the People in London*, first series, London, 1902.

Booth, William, *In Darkest England and the Way Out*, London, 1890.

Bosanquet, Helen, *Rich and Poor*, London, 1896.

Bosanquet, Helen, *The Standard of Life*, London, 1906.

Bosanquet, Helen, *The Family*, London, 1915.

Bosanquet, Helen (ed.), *Social Conditions in Provincial Towns*, London, 1912.

Cadbury, Edward; Matheson, M. Cecile, and Shann, George, *Women's Work and Wages: A Phase of Life in an Industrial City*, London, 1906.

Davies, Margaret Llewellyn (ed.), *Maternity Letters from Working Women* (collected by the Women's Co-operative Guild), first published 1915, Virago edition, London 1978.

Davies, Margaret Llewellyn (ed.), *Life as We Have Known It*, by Co-operative Working Women, first published in 1931, Virago edition, London, 1977.

Drake, Barbara, *Women in Trade Unions*, first published 1920, Virago edition, London, 1984.

Engels, Friedrich, *The Condition of the Working Class in England in 1844*, first published 1845, Oxford edition, 1958.

Freeman, Gwendolen, *The Houses Behind. Sketches of a Birmingham Back Street*, London, 1947.

Hill, Octavia, *Homes of the London Poor*, London, 1875.

Hutchins, B. L., *Women in Modern Industry*, London, 1915.

Keating, Peter (ed.), *Into Unknown England. Selections From the Social Explorers*, Glasgow, 1976.

Liddel, Mrs Edward, *A Shepherd of the Sheep. The Life Story of an English Parish Priest told by his Wife*, London, 1916.

Loane, Margaret, *The Queen's Poor: Life as they Find it in Town and Country*, London, 1905.

Loane, M. E., *From their Point of View (Short Papers on the Life of the Poor)*, London, 1908.

Loane, Margaret, *An Englishman's Castle*, London, 1909.

Loane, Margaret, *The Common Growth*, London, 1911.

London, Jack, *People of the Abyss*, first published 1903, Journeyman edition, 1977.

Macdonald, J. Ramsay, *Women in the Printing Trades, A Sociological Study*, London, 1904.

Martin, Anna, *The Married Working Woman: A Study*, London, 1911.

Masterson, G. F. G. (ed.), *Heart of the Empire. Discussions of Problems of Modern City Life in England*, London, 1901.

Mearns, Andrew, *The Bitter Cry of Outcast London. An Inquiry into the Conditions of the Abject Poor*, London, 1883.

Orwell, George, *The Road to Wigan Pier*, first published 1937, Penguin edition, 1987.

Patterson, Alexander, *Across the Bridges*, London, 1911.

Pember-Reeves, Mrs, *Round about a Pound a Week*, London, 1910.

Rice, Margery Spring, *Working Class Wives; Their Health and Conditions*, Harmondsworth, 1939.

Rook, Clarence, *The Hooligan Nights*, first published 1899, Oxford University Press edition, 1985.

Rowntree, B. Seebohm, *Poverty. A Study of Town Life*, London, 1903.

Sherard, Robert, *The White Slaves of England*, London, 1897.

Sherard, Robert, *The Child Slaves of England*, London, 1905.

Sherwell, Arthur, *Life in West London. A Study and a Contrast*, London, 1897.

Sims, George, *How the Poor Live*, London, 1883.

Snowden, Philip, *The Living Wage*, London, 1912.

The London School of Economics, *The New Survey of London Life and Labour*, London, 1930.

The University of Liverpool, *Social Survey of Liverpool*, London, 1934.

Tuckwell, Gertrude (ed.), *Women In Industry, from Seven Points of View*, London, 1908.

Cuming Walters, J., *Scenes in Slumland. Pen Pictures of the Black Spots in Birmingham*, articles reprinted from The Birmingham Daily Post, 1901.

Books

Anderson, Michael, *Family Structure in Nineteenth Century Lancashire*, London, 1971.

Benson, John, *The Penny Capitalists. A Study of Nineteenth-Century Working Class Entrepreneurs*, London, 1983.

Benson, John (ed.), *The Working Class in England, 1873–1914*, Kent, 1985.

Bott, Elizabeth, *Family and Social Networks*, second edition, London, 1968.

Burman, Sandra (ed.), *Fit Work for Women*, London, 1979.

Burnett, John, *Plenty and Want. A Social History of Diet in England from 1815 to the Present Day*. London, 1966.

Chamberlain, Mary, *Old Wives Tales. Their History, Remedies and Spells*, London, 1981.

Collis, Arthur and Poole, Vera E., *These Our Children*, London, 1950.

Flinn, M. W. and Snout, T. C. (eds.), *Essays in Social History*, Vol. I, Oxford, 1974.

Gillis, John, *Youth and History*, London, 1974.

Harrison, Brian, *Drink and the Victorians. The Temperance Question in England 1815–72*, London, 1971.

Hewitt, M., *Wives and Mothers in Victorian Industry*, London, 1958.

Hobsbawm, Eric, *Industry and Empire*, London, 1964.

Hoggart, Richard, *The Uses of Literacy. Aspects of Working Class Life with Special Reference to Publications and Entertainment*, London, 1957.

John, Angela V., *By the Sweat of Their Brow. Women Workers at Victorian Coal Mines*, London, 1980.

Kerr, Madeline, *The People of Ship Street*, London, 1958.

Lewenhak, Sheila, *Women and Trade Unions. An Outline History of Women in the British Trade Union Movement*, London and Tunbridge, 1977.

Lewis, Jane (ed.), *Labour and Love. Women's Experience of Home and Family 1850–1940*, Oxford and New York, 1986.

Liddington, Jill and Norris, Jill, *One Hand Tied Behind Us, The Rise of the Women's Suffrage Movement*, London, 1978.

Linklater, Andro, *An Unhusbanded Life, Charlotte Despord, Suffragette, and Sinn Feiner*, London, 1980.

McLaren, Angus, *Birth Control in Nineteenth Century England*, London, 1978.

McLeod, Hugh, *Class and Religion in the Late Victorian City*, London, 1974.

Malcolmsen, Patricia E., *English Laundresses. A Social History 1850–1930*, Chicago, 1986.

Marsh, D. C., *The Changing Social Structure of England and Wales 1811–1961*, London, 1967.

Meacham, Standish, *A Life Apart. The English Working Class 1890–1914*, London, 1977.

Mitchell, Geoffrey, *The Hard Way Up*, London, 1968.

Read, Donald, *England 1868–1914*, London, 1979.

Roberts, Elizabeth, *A Woman's Place. An Oral History of Working Class Women 1890–1914*, Oxford and New York, 1984.

Rose M. (ed.), *The Poor and the City: The English Poor Law in its Urban Context*, Leicester, 1985.

Stopes, Marie, *Married Love*, London, 1918.

Tebbut, Melanie, *Making Ends Meet. Pawnbroking and Working-Class Credit*, Leicester, 1983.

Thompson, Paul, *The Edwardians. The Remaking of British Society*, London, 1975.

Thompson, Edward, *The Making of The English Working Class*, Penguin, 1978.

Thane, Pat and Sutcliffe, Anthony, *Essays in Social History*, Vol. 2, Oxford, 1986.

Treble, J. H., *Urban Poverty in Britain 1830–1914*, London, 1983.

Vicinus, Martha (ed.), *Suffer and Be Still: Women in the Victorian Age*, Indiana, 1973.

Vicinus, Martha, *Independent Women, Work and Community for Single Women 1850–1920*, London, 1985.

Weller, P. J., *Town, City and Nation. England 1850–1914*, Oxford, 1983.

White, Jerry, *The Worst Street in North London. Campbell Bunk, Islington, Between the Wars*, London, 1986.

Young, Michael and Willmott, Peter, *Family and Kinship in East London*, London, 1977.

Articles in books

Davidoff, Leonore, 'Mastered for life: servant and wife in Victorian and Edwardian England' in Thane and Sutcliffe (eds.), *Essays in Social History*, Vol. 2.

Sigsworth, E. M. and Wyke, T. J., 'A study of Victorian prostitution and venereal disease' in Vicinus (ed.), *Independent Women, Work and Community for Single Women 1850–1920*.

Smith, F. B., 'Health' in Benson (ed.), *The Working Class in England, 1873–1914*.

Stearns, Peter N., 'Working class women in Britain, 1890–1914' in Vicinus (ed.), *Independent Women, Work and Community for Single Women 1850–1920*.

Titmuss, Richard, 'The position of women: some vital statistics' in Flinn and Smout (eds.), *Essays in Social History*, Vol. 1.

Woods, David, 'Community violence' in Benson (ed.), *The Working Class in England, 1873–1914*.

Articles

Kaye, Harvey, article on E. P. Thompson in *The Times Higher Educational Supplement*, 31 January 1986.

Maccaby, Eleanor G.; Johnson, Joseph B., and Church, Russel M., 'Community integration and the social control of juvenile delinquency' in *The Journal of Social Issues*, Vol. XIV, 1958, No. 3.

Miller, Walker B., 'Lower class culture as a generating milieu of gang delinquency' in *The Journal of Social Issues*, Vol. XIV, 1958, No. 3.

Oren, Laura, 'The welfare of women in labouring families, England 1860–1950' in *Feminist Studies*, Vol. I, Winter/Spring 1973.

Roberts, Elizabeth, 'Working class women in the North West' in *Oral History*, Vol. V, Autumn 1977.

Ross, Ellen, 'Fierce questions and taunts: married life in working-class London 1870–1914' in *Feminist Studies*, Vol. VIII, Winter 1982.

Ross, Ellen, 'Women's neighbourhood sharing in London before World War One' in *History Workshop*, Issue 15, Spring 1983.

Ross, Ellen, 'Not the sort that would sit on the doorstep': respectability in pre-World War I London neighbourhoods', *Working Class History*, No. 27, Spring 1985.

Unpublished theses

Chinn, Carl, 'The Anatomy of a working-class neighbourhood: West Sparkbrook 1871–1914', Birmingham University Ph.D., 1986.

Fiction

Allen, Walter, *All in a Lifetime*, first published 1959, Hogarth edition, 1986.

Douglas, John, *A Walk down Summer Lane*, Warwick, 1977.

Gaskell, Elizabeth, *North and South*, 1855.

Gissing, George, *The Nether World*, first published 1889, Everyman edition, 1982.

Greenwood, Walter, *Love on the Dole*, first published 1933, Penguin edition, 1986.

Keating, P. J., *The Working Classes in Victorian Fiction*, London, 1971.

Morrison, Arthur, *A Child of The Jago*, London, 1896.

Morrison, Arthur, *Tales of Mean Streets*, London, 1906.

Murray, David Christie, *A Capful o' Nails*, first published 1896, Black Country Society Edition, 1977.

Index

abortion, 70, 148–9
Abortion Law Reform Society, 148
Acorn, George, 49, 53, 58, 102, 105, 135, 163
Acts of Parliament: Factories and Workshop Act, 1901, 102–3; Midwives Act, 1902, 139; National Insurance Act, 1911, 140
Adler, Nettie, 68
affection, 47, 150; lack of, 46–9; *see also* love
Allen, Walter, 7, 31, 163
Alsace Street, 38
Amalgamated Society of Engineers, 87
Anderson, Michael, 37
Aston, 25, 43, 121
Aston Manor, 88
autobiographies, working-class, 8–9, 45, *passim*

back-to-back houses, 26, 41, 50, 71, 111, 124, 126
Balsall Heath, 28, 134
Balsall Heath Times, The, 25
barmaids, 106–7
Bass, Reverend T.J., 50–1, 103, 127, 150–1, 157–9
beer houses, *see* drink
Bell, Lady, 20–1, 34, 58, 104, 139, 155
Benson, John, 108–10, 113, 137
Bermondsey, 18, 48
Besant, Walter, 10
Bethnal Green, 25–6, 28, 47, 71
Bingley Hall, 81
Birmingham, 1, 4–5, 9, 14, 16, 24, 26, 28, 32, 34, 37, 39–41, 43, 47–8, 50, 53, 55, 62, 65–6, 70, 73–4, 76–82, 86–8, 90–2, 94, 96–7, 99–101, 103–7, 110–13, 115, 117, 119–21, 123–6, 128–9, 134–7, 139–40, 143–4, 146, 149–50, 152–3, 155–6, 158–63
Birmingham Coroner's Court, 141, 150
Birmingham Daily Gazette, 125
Birmingham Daily Mail, 80
Birmingham Daily Post, 91
Birmingham Journal, 157
Birmingham Women's Settlement, 80, 118, 123
birth, 139–41; *see also* maternal mortality
birth control, 134, 138, 141, 147–9; *see also* abortion
birth rate, 134–5, 138
Black, Clementina, 47, 58–9, 94–6, 99, 104–5, 118, 131–2, 139
Black Country, the, 47, 74, 103; *see also* Cradley Heath
Bolton, 46
bookmakers, 41
Booth, Charles, 2–3, 10, 72, 78, 88, 93–5, 97, 99, 118, 120, 161
Booth, William, 6–7
Bosanquet, Helen, 45, 51, 56, 96, 102, 118
Bradford, 75
Bray, Reginald, 150
breast feeding, *see* infant mortality
brewis, *see* sop
Brick Lane, 71
Bristol, 38
broxy, 65
Bryant and May, 89, 102
bugs, 127–8
Bull Ring, 70, 113
Burnett, John, 5, 8, 39, 47, 61–2, 64, 67

Burnley, 108
butchers, 65–6

Cadbury, E., 86, 88, 90–1, 94, 98,
    102, 104–5
cadging, *see* charity
cag-mag, 65
Campbell Bunk, 37, 78, 154, 162
Carnegie Infant Welfare Centre,
    137
census, 1901, 85, 96, 110
chainmakers, 65, 103, 139
Chamberlain, Mary, 38, 40, 149
Charities Organising Committee,
    80
charity, 54–5, 80–1,123
charring, 105–6, 110
Chelsea, 51
Chesterfield, 123
Chew, Ada Nield, 15, 55, 59, 98
Chew, Doris Nield, 15
child-minding, 107–8
children's wages, 67–8
children's work: industrial, 68–9;
    irregular, 69–70
churching, 143–4
cleanliness, 82, 122–31; lack of,
    122, 129–31
clothes, 30, 115, 119–20, 166
Collet, Clara E., 88
Collis, Arthur, 122, 130
communal control, 41–4, 71, 129–
    32, 144–7, 152–3, 165
communal self-help, 30–1, 34–5,
    37, 39–40, 77; *see also* child-
    minding; didlum clubs; folk
    medicine; fostering; granny-
    rearing; midwives, unofficial;
    laying-out; trips; wreaths
communities, 13, 21, 40, 72, 129–31
contraception, *see* birth control
cooking utensils, 63
Cookson, Catherine, 31, 35, 37, 40–3,
    63, 107, 112, 152
co-operative stores, 74
corner shops, 73–4
cost of living, 55–8
Country Holiday Schemes, 123

Cradley Heath, 65, 103
Crawford, Sir William, 61
Crooks, Will, 68

daughters, eldest, 31–3
Davidoff, Leonore, xii, 21, 142
Davies, Margaret Llewellyn, 138
Dayuss, Kathleen, 14, 30, 35, 40–1,
    49, 82, 108, 120, 127–8, 138, 143,
    146, 156, 159, 161–2
debt, 72; *see also* money-lending;
    pawnbroking; Provident Clothing
    Company cheques; rent; strap
deference, 106
didlum clubs, 79
diet, 60–2; *see also* meals
divorce, 158
doctors, 140
domestic service, 85, 106
Douglas, John, 48, 127, 160
Drake, Barbara, 57
drink, 66, 117–21
Duddeston, 134
Dudley Road Hospital, 137
Duncan, Dr, 50, 101, 131
Durham, 75

East End, 10, 33, 46, 77, 88–9
East Jarrow, 31; *see also* North-
    East England
Edgbaston, 134–5
Educational Census Books, 27
endogamy, 27–9
Engels, Friedrich, 85
environment, *see* slums
extended families, 27, 36, 107–8

factory girls, 93–4
family size, 3
fatalism, *see* realism
fatherhood, 16–17
female solidarity, 22; *see also*
    communal self-help; extended
    family; neighbourliness
feminine ideal, 51, 165
feminists, xii, 15, 85, 98
First World War, 10; *see also*
    social change

Floodgate Street, 80
Foakes, Grace, 8, 46, 62, 121, 159
Foley, Alice, 46, 54, 146, 160
folk medicine, 40
food, *see* brewis; broxy; butchers; cag-mag; diet; offal; meals; milk; slink; sop; spec
food purchase, 64
Forrester, Helen, 29–30, 35, 59, 64, 94, 129, 161, 164
fostering, 34–7; *see also* granny-rearing
Freeman, Gwendolen, 5, 25, 35–6, 46, 54, 149
funeral suppers, 39

gaffers, *see* matriarchs
Gamble, Rose, 51
Garrison Lane, 24, 41
Gaskell, Mrs, 94
Gillis, John, 68
girls in factories, 93
Gissing, George, 6–7, 88, 113
Glasgow, 123
Golding, Rose, 120
Golding, Tom, 82
Goodman, Albert, 38
gossip, 44, 116
grandmothers, 29–31, 107; and dress, 30
granny-rearing, 30–1
Green, Benny, 7
Greenwood, Walter, 55, 76–8, 127

half-timers, 68
Hall, Edith, 126, 146
Handsworth, 88
Harborne, 134–5
Harding, Arthur, 33, 71, 77–8, 80, 90, 103, 113, 121
Harrison, Brian, 118
Haw, George, 68
health, 136–9
health, infants, 100–1; *see also* Carnegie Infant Welfare Centre; infant mortality
health, women, 20, 133–4, 138–41
health visitors, 82, 122–5, 136

Heathfield Road, 137
Heywood, Wyn, 47, 50, 53, 107, 145–6, 153, 159
hidden matriarchy, *see* matriarchy
Hill, Dr, 86, 124, 151
Hobsbawn, Eric, 10
Hoggart, Richard, 94
home work, 101–3, 105–8
hooligans, 29
household management, 58–9, 63–7; *see also* late-night shopping; meals
housekeeping, 52–9
Hoxton, 26, 35
huckster's shops, *see* corner shops
husbands, 17, 52–4; and housework, 16, 54; and money, 53; *see also* patriarchy
Hutchins, B.L., 98–9, 118
Hyndman, H.M., 2

illegitimacy, 31, 145–6
incest, 41, 151–3
Industrial Revolution, 85
infant mortality, 100, 135–7, 150; *see also* overlaying
Inspector of Nuisances, 123
intermarriage, *see* endogamy
Ireland, 54
Islington, 37, 64, 94

Jamaica Row, 65
Jarrow, 120
Jasper, A.P., 26, 33, 45, 54, 121, 163–4
Jews, 40
John, Angela V., xii

Kaye Harvey, xi
Keating, Peter, 6
Kerr, Madeline, 24, 34, 38, 141
Kings Norton, 88

Labour, 68
Labour Gazette, 108
Ladypool Road, 53, 65
Ladywood, 82
Lambeth, 16, 29, 52, 54, 57, 79, 115

Lancashire, 37, 68, 74, 85, 89–90, 92; *see also* North-West England
Lannigan, Jack, 67
late-night shopping, 66
laundries, 110
laying-out, 39, 105
Layton, Mrs, 47, 53
Leeds, 75
Leek, 59
Lewisham, 28
Liddel, Mrs, 120, 150, 157, 161
Liddington, Jill, xii, 89–90, 92, 107
Linklater, Andro, xii
Liverpool, 17, 24, 29, 38, 60, 64, 74, 76, 94, 96, 123
Loane, M.E., 16, 43, 52, 147, 162
London, xii, 2, 10, 26, 28, 74, 78, 90, 93, 95, 97, 104–5, 121, 126, 130, 156
London, Jack, 6, 12
love, 16, 156–7; *see also* affection
Luton, 126

Macclesfield, 59
Macdonald, J. Ramsay, 95
McLeod, Hugh, 28, 143
Malcolmsen, Patricia, 110–11
malnutrition, 50, 138
Manchester, 55, 74, 76, 94, 99, 124, 127
mangles, 112–13
marriage, 17, 155
married women, divisions amongst, 94–6
married women working, 95–6; numbers, 96–7; opposition to, 97–8; wages, 97
Martin, Anna, 7, 21, 36, 41, 59, 163
Masterman, C.F.G., 1, 7, 34, 150
maternal mortality, 140–1
maternity, 50
maternity feeding centres, 137
Matheson, M. Cecile, 86
matriarchs, 29–34, 37–8, 40–4, 46, 77, 79–80, 105, 107, 129; and strength, 40–2, 160–4; *see also* women and masculinity
matriarchy, 23, 29–34, 44, 165
matrilocality, 24
Mayhew, Henry, 6

Meacham, Standish, xii
meals, 15, 50, 53–5, 59, 62–3, 71
Mearns, Andrew, 126
Means Test, the, 81–2
Medical Officer of Health of Birmingham, 9, 17–18, 50, 86, 99–100, 121
Medical Officer of Health of Newcastle, 61–2, 138
menstruation, 143; *see also* churching
middle class, *see* social explorers
Middlesborough, 20, 104, 155
midwives, 139–40; unofficial, 38–9
milk, 63
missionaries to the urban poor, 84
money-lenders, 78–9
money-lending, 77–9
monkey run, 118
morality, *see* communal control
Morrison, Arthur, 7, 71
Moseley, 70
Moseley and Kings Heath Journal, The, 56
mothers, 12, 17; and constancy, 18–19; and daughters, 23, *see also* matrilocality; and devotion of children, 45–6, 68; and devotion to children, 45–6, 49–51; as failures, 18, 56; and financial control, 51, *see also* household management; and politics, 22; position of, 21; and power, 13, 22, 52; role of, 19–22, 26–7; and sons, 24, 26, 27, 29; upper and middle-class, 19; upper working-class, 19
Mothers' Union, 115, 118
munitions workers, 146
Murray, David Christie, 47
music hall songs, 12

nailmakers, 47
National Association for the Promotion of Social Science, 85
National Union of Brass Workers and Metal Mechanics, 87
neighbourliness, *see* communal self-help

'Nichol, The', 71
night work, 101
Norris, Jill, xii, 89–90, 92, 107
North-East England, 37; *see also*
    East Jarrow; Jarrow
Northumberland, 75
North-West England, 35; *see also*
    Lancashire; Liverpool;
    Manchester; Preston
Notting Hill, 28
Nottinghamshire, 47

offal, 65
old wives, *see* midwives, unofficial
oral history, 9, *passim*
ostracisation, *see* communal control
outcasts, 34
out work, 101, 103
overlaying, 150

Paddington, 28, 54, 121, 128, 153, 161
Pall Mall Gazette, 110
parish relief, 81–3
parochialism, *see* streets, culture of
patriarchy, 12–16, 21, 23, 44, 46,
    114, 141, 148, 164
Patterson, Alexander, 18, 32, 45–6,
    51, 128, 150, 156, 165
Patterson, Emma, 89
pawn of wedding rings, 75–6
pawnbroking, 74–7
pawnbroking agents, 77
Penns Lane, 137
penny capitalism, 35, 108–10
Perry, Margaret, 47
Perry Barr, 135
physical deterioration, 6–7, 18
physical efficiency, 2
Police-Aided Association for
    Clothing Children, 81
Police Courts, 124
Poole, Vera G., 122, 130
Poor Man's Lawyer Association,
    the, 118
Poor Person's Divorce, 158
Poplar, 68
Potteries, the, 74; *see also* Stoke
poverty, causes of, 2–3

poverty, culture of, 4; *see also*
    streets, culture of
poverty cycle, 3
poverty line, 2, 52, 60
pregnancy, 136–7, *see also* birth
    control; health; women
Preston, 113
prostitutes, 34, 120, 122, 146–7,
    149, 151
Provident Clothing Company
    cheques, 79
Public Health Committee, 140
public houses, *see* drink
Pype Hayes Hall, 137

Pember-Reeves, Mrs, 16, 52, 54,
    57–58, 115
Rag Market, 113–4
realism, 164–5
Registry Offices and Training
    Homes, 106
religion, 39
rent, 72–3
reports: Birmingham Trades for
    Women and Girls, 1914, 91;
    Report of the Inter-Depart-
    mental Committee on Physical
    Deterioration, 1904, 7, 61;
    Report of the Medical Officer
    of Health of Birmingham, 1904,
    99–100; Report of the Medical
    Officer of Health of Birming-
    ham, 1906, 107, 131; Report of
    the Medical Officer of Health
    of Birmingham into *The*
    Industrial Employment of
    Married Women and Infantile
    Mortality, 1909, 50, 96–7, 99,
    139; Report of the Medical
    Officer of Health of Birming-
    ham, 1914, 100; Report of the
    Registrar General, 1905, 134;
    Report on Trade Unions, 1896, 89
Rhondda, the, 135, 137
Rhyl, 41
Rice, Margery Spring, 20, 116, 133
Roberts, Elizabeth, xii, 21–2, 35,
    37, 39, 109, 113, 144, 148, 152

Roberts, Robert, 8, 14, 16, 30, 33, 39, 42–3, 73, 90–1, 104, 115, 121, 127, 141, 147, 149, 152, 163–4
Robertson, Dr John, 17, 50, 56, 80, 96, 107, 125, 129–30, 134, 136, 141, 148, 150, 155
Rodaway, Angela, 9, 64, 76
Rook, Clarence, 7, 29
Ross, Ellen, xii, 2, 35, 121, 129, 165
Roth, Dr, 148
rough justice, *see* communal control
Rowntree, B. Seebohm, 2, 60, 115

St Bartholomew's ward, 136
St George's ward, 50
St Laurence's parish, 50, 150, 153, 157
St Martin's ward, 50
St Stephen's ward, 134
Salford, 8, 14, 16, 30, 63, 65, 67, 92, 104, 120–1, 127
Salisbury Street, 38
Samuels, Raphael, 33
savings, *see* didlum clubs
Scannel, Dolly, 46–7, 142
schools, 68; and attendance, 69
Second World War, 10
Selly Oak Hospital, 137
sex, 141–5, 148
sexual ignorance, 143–5
Shambles, the, 65
Shann, G., 86
Sheffield, 75
Shelton Street, 161
Sherard, Robert, 65, 69, 103, 138–9
Sherwell, Arthur, 97
Ship Street, 24, 26, 87, 141
Sigsworth, E.M., 151
Sims, George, 6
slink, 65
slums, 5–8, 124–8, *passim*
slum clearance, 130, 135, 137–8
Smethwick, 88
Smith, Dr Edward, 61–2
Smith, F.B., 137
social conservatism, 166
social change, 165–6
Social Democratic Federation, 2

social explorers, 1–8, 10, *passim*
social history, xi–xii, 9, *passim*
Social Survey of Liverpool, 17
socialists, 15
Society for the Prevention of Cruelty to Children, 122
sop, 61–2
Sparkbrook, *see* West Sparkbrook
spec, 63
Stearns, Peter N., xii, 59
Steedman, Carolyn, 48
Stoke, 38
Stopes, Marie, 148
strap, 73–4
streets, culture of the, 23–4, 116
Studley Street, 24, 27–8, 31, 35–7, 38, 41–2, 44, 63, 69–70, 73, 75–8, 110, 147, 153
suffragettes, 7, 85; *see also* feminists
suffragists, 92–3
Summer Lane, 5, 25, 48, 80
Sumner Report, 60
sweated industries, 86, 102–3, 110

Tebbutt, Melanie, 44, 74–8
textiles, 85, 89–93
theft, 70–1
Thompson, Edward, xi
Trades Boards, 110
trips, 41
Tuckwell, Gertrude, 68

urban poor: 1–11; Birmingham, 1, 4–5, 124–5; London, xii, 2, 10; York, 2–3, *passim*

Vicinus, Martha, xii
violence, *see* communal control; wife beating; women fighting

wakes, 39
Walters, J. Cuming, 125–6, 129
wardrobe dealers, 113–14
Warwickshire, 74
washing, 67, 109–13; *see also* mangles
Weavers' Amalgamation, 89

West London, 97
West Sparkbrook, 4, 25, 27–8, 121
Wheatley, Mr, 84
White, Jerry, 37, 78, 154, 162
Whitehouse Street, 25, 160
widows, 147, 156, 159
wife beating, 156–61
Wilkins, W., 99
Williams, Lady, 138
women and independence, 84–5, 98, 114
women and leisure, 115–18; *see also* drink; Mothers' Union; monkey run
women and masculinity, 23–4, 91–2, 111, 160–4; *see also* matriarchs; women fighting
women fighting, 161–4
women, working-class, xii, *passim*
women's history, xi–xii, *passim*
Women's Co-operative Guild, 47, 95, 108, 115
Women's Group on Public Welfare, 10
women's trade unions, 87–90
Women's Trade Union League, 89
women's wages, 86–8, 91–2, 102–4, 107, 110, 117

women's work, 85; Birmingham, 86–8, 90–2; clean work, 91–2; East End, 89–90; french polishers, 90; hierarchy, 90–4; hours, 92; industrial, 85–6, 90, 117; irregular, 104, 107; Lancashire, 89–93; necessity of, 88; numbers, 85; opposition to, 87, 90; reasons for, 98–9, rough work, 91–2; support for, 98, 101; *see also* barmaids; charring; child-minding; domestic service; home work; night work; sweated industries; wardrobe dealers; washing
Woodward, Kathleen, 48
workhouses, 60, 114, 159
working class: Birmingham, 1; income, 1; London, 2; stratification, 1–4; 'traditional', 10; York, 2
wreaths, 40
Wyke, T.J., 151

yards, 41
York, 2, 60
Yorkshire, 74, 99
Young and Willmott, 24–5, 27